THE WINNING POINT

How to Master
the Mindset of Champions

THE WINNING POINT

How to Master the Mindset of Champions

Loren Fogelman

ISBN: 978-0-9852900-0-9

Library of Congress Control Number: 2012938537

First Edition
Printed in the United States
10 9 8 7 6 5 4 3 2 1

To Steven Fogelman, my husband, best friend, and number-one supporter. I am so appreciative and blessed to have him by my side.

Table of Contents

introduction

The last time you failed, what happened? Did you get discouraged? Did you beat yourself up? Did you consider throwing in the towel?

If so, you might have missed an opportunity for a breakthrough.

The truth is failure is necessary for success. If you're not failing, you're not taking risks. And if you're not taking risks, you're not going to reach your peak performance.

The goal is not to avoid failure, but to approach it as an opportunity in disguise.

Exactly how to do that is one of the many tools I'll teach you in this book.

As you will see, I walk my talk. When it feels right I will go against the grain and be bold. It's probably one of the reasons I felt like a black sheep as I was growing up.

In fact, if you had told me at age 12 that one day I would be teaching athletes how to reach their maximum potential, I would have said you were crazy. Throughout my school years, I was always one of the last kids picked for team sports. I wasn't fast enough, tall enough or strong enough. In fact, physical education (P.E.) was torturous. I was much more at home in the library.

Like many kids who are not natural athletes, I didn't realize there was more to the game than what you were born with. I also didn't realize that the competitive fire could be kindled, emerge suddenly as it did, taking me by surprise in my forties.

That's how old I was when I traded the mall for the outdoors after moving cross-country from Miami, Florida, to Ashland, Oregon. Over the years, I *had* overcome my aversion to physical activity: I exercised vigorously, for a year I played on a pickup volleyball team, and during my first pregnancy, I swam a mile every day, but competitive sports was new.

Given the passion sports has become in my life and work, it's surprising to my clients to learn that I am a relative newbie. I got into sports to challenge myself physically and mentally and to share activities with my family. Fortunately, when we moved from the city to the country, our backyard offered a rich variety of seasonal outdoor activities.

The kids signed up for a learn-to-ski program in our community, and my husband and I volunteered. I tagged along on the beginner lessons, learning to ski downhill, doing pizza's side-by-side with the eight-year-olds. It wasn't a lot of fun in the beginning; I wasn't naturally good at it, but I kept at it, every week, and got better.

When the weather warmed up we took a rowing class, which I didn't find much fun either at first. The learning curve was pretty steep, but I stuck with it.

It wasn't long, though, before I was hooked on sports. I like things that I can focus on very intensely. When I'm that focused on what I'm doing any worries just go away. Also, at the time, Steve and I were running our own counseling agency with eleven employees, and sports gave us an escape from the day-to-day stressors of the business.

To my participation in sports, I applied a personal philosophy I've always used on myself and with my clients. I believe that I have not been given any challenges in my life I can't rise up to and overcome—even if I've chosen those challenges myself. We all can overcome incredible obstacles as long as we don't give up.

Over the course of four years I transitioned from seasonal to year-round recreational rowing to stepping up to the Women's Racing Team. At 44 years old, for the first time in my life, I was part of a competitive team.

Actually, my first regatta was a fluke. I was still a recreational rower at the time, and a woman who was supposed to be in the race asked me if I would take her seat. I had no real understanding of what that entailed, but said, "Sure." I was so naïve I didn't even know I was supposed to be nervous.

It was a small, fun regatta—we were racing in costumes—and it was a sprint race, so it was 1,000 meters, and it was an eight, which means there were eight rowers in the boat.

Having never prepared for a race before, I had no idea how to manage my energy, and it was tough. There's no rest and recovery period in rowing, and if you're in a boat with seven other people, no matter how tired you are, you can't quit, so you row your heart out the whole race. Four minutes can be a very long time.

Still, I loved it, and the race planted the seed of my movement to the women's racing team, which I did a few months later.

Again, I wasn't seeking competition per se. I joined the team because I wanted a greater physical challenge and to be among a group of rowers who were more committed to a higher level of training and the sport than the recreational rowers were. Also, by that time, I loved rowing and wanted to do it as much as I could. I started training six days a week on the lake, changing my work schedule so I could row in the morning.

Some people want to meditate or drink coffee in the morning, I wanted to row. And why not? I got to go out on this beautiful lake with gorgeous surroundings, where I might see an eagle fishing for its breakfast or a deer swimming across the lake.

Rowing changed my life. And, as I started racing, I was surprised to discover a competitor within me. Get me in a boat at a race, even a mock race, and I row to win!

Winning, however, wasn't a slam-dunk for me. I still wasn't the tallest or the strongest, but I kept at it and stretched myself in ways I didn't know I could.

Like any athlete who makes a similar transition from recreational to competitive sports, I discovered that competitive sports demanded I face some fears, limiting thoughts and beliefs, which were holding me back from reaching my peak performance.

Luckily, I had some strategies for approaching that. Since 1985 I had helped my clients overcome their fears and change the belief systems that held them back at work or in their relationships.

I had developed a reputation for quick results—sometimes after only one session—so I was determined to give myself the benefit of my own skill. I adopted a "no-excuses" approach and began working on my "champion mindset."

One of the biggest obstacles holding me back was that old one from when I was 12: my perceived physical limitations. It's true that the physical requirements of competitive rowing were a big challenge for me, and I've had to make a number of technical adjustments to compensate for my height (I'm 4'11"), but focusing on those limitations was negatively affecting my performance.

During that first year of competitive rowing, I was also transitioning out of the counseling business I ran with Steve and opening my own business, which eventually became Expert Sports Performance. Both of those actions were pushing me out of my comfort zone, and I was facing limiting beliefs I didn't even know I had.

One of the things that helped me move forward was deciding to "become comfortable being uncomfortable," a business marketing concept, but one that I have lived by since I was a little girl. I decided to apply it to sports, embracing the motto: "If it's uncomfortable then I ought to be doing it."

My motto gave me permission not just to face my fears, but to actively seek them out so I could clear them. I committed to doing whatever was necessary to work toward my sports-related goals as well as my business-related desires.

I was determined to break those limiting, self-imposed barriers, part of which was focusing on my physical limitations.

Your Mental Game and Focus

In order to overcome my perceived limitations and continue to improve, I had to change my mental game and focus. By "mental game" I mean my beliefs and perceptions. I needed to become aware of my limiting beliefs. I also began reframing obstacles into opportunities. To "reframe" means to change the way you perceive something. You see it through a different set of lenses, from a different perspective.

One opportunity to do that came about as I faced having to take the indoor rowing test, which was required every year in order to be able to row on the racing team. It was something I dreaded.

The angst I had about taking the test was only adding to my struggle. I had thoughts like, "I can't do this." Also, the first time I took the test, I got halfway into it and was thinking, "Oh, my God, how can I do this for another two-and-a-half minutes!"

Those thoughts didn't help, so the next year I decided to train with a world-class rower, Andy Baxter, to improve my technique and tap into his winning mindset. While training with him physically, I also worked on my mental game, dredging up anything and everything that was getting in my way.

Using the tools I used on my business clients, I changed my mindset—the way I was thinking. Instead of saying, "I can't do it," I started saying, "I can do anything for two-and-a-half minutes."

That simple shift to "I can do anything for X amount of minutes" had a profound effect and helped with races as well. My focus went from *I can't* to *Yeah, I can! Bring it on!*

I actively used visualizations and tapping (EFT—Emotional Freedom Techniques—a very simple technique I'll explain in Chapter 6. Also, since memories are reinforced through emotion and we tend to remember jingles, I created some jingles around rowing to help with my mindset shift.

Those techniques created a paradigm shift—which is the

purpose of the work I do with my clients. It's not about adding to what they do, my work is about clearing the gunk, getting rid of the negative clutter, those self-defeating thoughts, and changing the impact their story has on them, so that they have the clarity of, *Yes! I can do that.*

If you combine my method with physical conditioning you'll discover the quick and significant results that training both physically and emotionally/mentally can bring. It's like that equation 1 + 1 = 3. Together the two modalities create dynamic results far greater than either could alone.

What Is Possible for You

Sometimes we create a goal for ourselves that is so big or meaningful we talk ourselves out of it. Because what if it doesn't happen? What does that say about us? What does that mean?

If you have the goal, you can accomplish it. As I said before, you're not given any challenges you can't overcome. Therefore it becomes a matter of perspective. Consider the underdogs who were told, "You've gotta be kidding, you want to do that?" and then they went on to defy the odds. They did so because they were so committed to their vision that they actively looked for opportunities and they saw obstacles as just another challenge to get through, whereas another person might walk away from their dream.

A perfect example is the four-minute mile.

Up until the mid-1950s, physiologists said that humans couldn't run a four-minute mile. They said our hearts weren't made for it and a runner could die, trying to do it. Roger Bannister, a 25-year-old medical student at Oxford didn't believe that and started training to run the four-minute mile. Because he could envision it and was dedicated to making it happen, on May 6, 1954, before a crowd of 1,000 people, he ran the mile in 3 minutes, 59.4 seconds.

Forty-six days later, another runner, John Landy, did the same. Three years later, 16 other runners had achieved the same feat.

As that story shows, limiting beliefs are not just held by the individual. They can be shared by us all and perceived as truth when they're actually just based upon perception and rationale. Now there was some logic to back up that particular belief, but, as I'll show you later, logic only goes so far.

When Roger Bannister ran the four-minute mile, he broke a barrier for *everyone* in his field.

In this book, I'm going to show you how to break the barriers in your own mind. I'll share with you simple yet powerful ways to shift the way you're thinking so you can be freed from the doubts, worries and fears that are holding you back.

Some of what you read may sound strange at first. It may sound too simple, too easy. I was skeptical too at first that something as simple as "tapping" could have an effect, but I tested it and the results spoke for itself.

I'm going to close with that story because it illustrates how small changes in thinking can have far-reaching results.

How EFT Changed My Life and Work

Before I became hooked on sports and went out on my own, I felt that some nugget was missing from my counseling practice, so I started exploring other approaches. When I became aware of energy psychology, it felt like the missing link.

Despite my initial enthusiasm, at the first EFT workshop I attended I was a complete skeptic. It was so far removed from anything I'd ever seen before, and I just couldn't see how tapping on your body while saying some words could work. But I didn't fully discount it and took the manual home.

Several months later, when we were going to visit my family in Florida for the holidays, I decided to try EFT on myself to curb my desire for sugar and chocolate—which I'd struggled with all my life. Every morning and afternoon for ten days, I went into the bathroom, so no one could see, and I "tapped." Two things came out of it. I ate much less chocolate and sugar than usual and, to my astonishment, my allergies disappeared. Growing up in Florida, I had lived on allergy medications, and when I used to visit, within one or two days, I'd be miserable. But this time, I had no allergy symptoms at all.

On the plane on the way back home, I decided that I wasn't going to eat chocolate or sugar anymore—my desire was just not there—and I haven't had sweets since 2006. That was amazing to me at the time, because, as I said, controlling my sugar intake had been a lifelong struggle, and being able to walk away from it so easily was surprising.

Later I learned that the foods you crave are an energetic allergy. Because I was tapping for the energetic allergy to chocolate, without realizing it, I was actually correcting my energy system around allergies in general. Also, since 2006, I haven't had any allergy symptoms at all.

After those results, I started doing EFT with a client, an actor who wanted to move up to better parts in his company. I found that a core incident holding him back occurred in his senior year during a football game when the ball was thrown to him and slipped through his fingers. It was the final seconds of the final game of the season, and he was blamed when the team lost the district title. As a result of our work together on this one incident, his fear of "missing a line" went away. He started to have more acting work than he could handle, *and* his golf game improved.

Inspired by those results, I tried EFT with an elderly lady in our rowing club, who was experiencing a lot of anxiety before competing. I helped her see it was windy conditions she feared. We worked with it, and after only one session, were able to get to the heart of her anxiety and completely eliminate it. The following weekend at the regatta she faced her worst nightmare, windy conditions, and reported no anxiety while waiting for the start of the race.

Once I experienced those results, I knew I had to share what I'd learned. I started to work with other athletes, talented and dedicated individuals and teams, who were holding themselves back, thinking they just had to tough it out, and who didn't realize that change can occur easily.

Since those early results, I have worked with thousands of private clients, spoken in front of groups, gotten great results on radio shows, and developed my Winner's Circle Method, which I'm teaching you in this book.

Here's the bottom line: You don't have to struggle. And you already know how to be great.

My work is about helping you get past your barriers, achieve freedom, and easily access your winning potential. I won't be happy until you reach your top goal, whether that's the Olympics, professional sports, or getting ranked at the state, national, or world level.

If you have that goal, you can get there. So let's get started.

Part One

Think Like a Winner

Chapter 1

Where Do You Want to Be?

How big is your vision? What goal have you set for yourself? Do you want to be ranked or compete in the Olympics or rise to the top of your sport as a professional? Do you daydream about it? Do you see yourself winning?

I have good news for you. If you can dream about being at the top, then it is possible to actually be there. I'm not talking about hocus pocus or magic. I'm talking about the power of your mind and the strength of your convictions.

The first step to realizing your vision is to learn how to think like a winner. Your champion mindset will not only boost your confidence, but give you an edge over the competition.

How a Champion Mindset Pays Off

When you're competing at the elite level, there is a small margin between the best athlete and the rest. Since success is 90% mindset—which means, how you think—it's clear that a champion mindset can make the difference.

Too many athletes neglect their mental training, which leads to wasted energy and poor focus. When you're competing, you need all the energy and concentration you can muster for winning results. You want to be laser focused on your goal, the job you set out to do. Expending energy on distractions, such as self-critical thoughts, is wasting your valuable resource.

Champion mindset training begins with getting rid of the

gunk, understanding where those negative thoughts come from and working to free yourself from their grip. Yes, it is possible, but training is needed. A champion mindset is learned.

As you train, you gain mental and emotional endurance and become stronger, as well as more flexible, responsive and resilient. Those are the key ingredients for going the distance. Athletes lacking in these qualities only go so far before negative thoughts creep in and stop them. But when your focus is strong and unwavering and you can do what is necessary without taking the situation personally, you will see significant results during competitions.

We've been told about the importance of muscle memory. Repetition strengthens the path, or neuropathways, that electrical signals follow, which in turn causes muscle groups to respond. The same thing happens with mental training. Your new techniques build neuropathways in the brain that become second nature when it's time to compete.

Why Mental Training Is Necessary

Many people say they want to be at the top of their game, but it doesn't happen. Why? Underneath their words, in their subconscious, are values or beliefs that are contradictory to being a winner. These beliefs are often unknown to you because they were adopted from the adults surrounding you before you were able to reason, before about age 7.

We also form subconscious beliefs from the experiences we have. For instance, if a child is made fun of by the neighborhood kids during sports, the child develops certain beliefs about himself. He may believe he's slow or awkward. Even if he later becomes an athlete, in part to prove the neighbor kids wrong, those old beliefs are still underneath, interfering with his every attempt to excel.

So he may say all the right things to himself, but he also holds himself back, gets distracted easily, or gets injured, and he doesn't understand why.

When your words, your conscious thoughts are not in alignment with the values or beliefs in your subconscious incongruency occurs, a struggle develops. The subconscious mind always wins a struggle.

On the other hand, when your values and beliefs match the things you say there is congruency, and you can then excel at whatever you choose to do. Haven't you ever been determined to do something your way even though everyone else had doubts, and you succeeded? That's congruency. One of the tricks for consistent congruency, which I'll show you in subsequent chapters, is to ferret out the beliefs you're not aware of so that you can work to be free of them.

Your Big Why

In the rest of this chapter, we're going to focus on strengthening your conscious mind, the thoughts you *are* aware of. Part of that is encouraging you to dream big. Another part is to discover your motivation to excel. What is your *Big Why*?

In other words, what drives you to compete? Why are you committed to reaching the top of your game? I want you to understand the driving force motivating you to keep going even if someone else tells you to quit.

That motivation is different for each person.

External and Internal Motivators

Often people get into sports because someone encouraged them, their parents signed them up for little league or soccer. Originally they had an *external motivator*—the motivation was outside of them rather than within. Then as they got more and more into the sport, they developed their own love for the game or got other personal satisfaction out of it. They developed their own *internal motivation*, which means that they were connected to *why* they were playing their sport or competing.

External factors can get you started in sports, but they don't have enough power to keep you committed if, for instance, those factors are not truly aligned with your values. An example is the athlete playing football because his dad played football and his father expects that from him, but deep in his heart he would rather be playing music. Eventually, he's going to quit football.

External motivations also aren't strong enough to keep you going when circumstances become difficult. You may be a natural athlete and get awards, but if you never connect to your internal motivation, once your external motivation is gone and you hit a rough patch, you will likely walk away.

Internal motivation, on the other hand, promotes long-lasting success. Your Big Why is an internal motivator. When you connect to your Big Why, you are driven to excel, ready to go the distance despite obstacles that appear along the way. It's as though you have a flame burning inside of you, igniting you to reach your goal.

Many athletes love to compete. A client of mine lives to bring home a medal. Bringing home that medal is what drives him to do the training required to compete in tournaments.

My internal motivation is to be the best I can be. I tend to be highly driven and I always want to be a student first, increasing what I know and stretching myself. That was my motivation for learning to ski and row and eventually competing in rowing.

What drives you in your sport? What keeps you going when you face obstacles?

Connecting with Your Big Why Is Crucial

If you don't connect with your Big Why, eventually you will give up, get injured, or claim that your dream was not "meant to be."

For instance, if you have a coach or parents who are critical of you, and you're not connected to your Big Why, eventually you can get beaten down by the criticism, believe in their negativity and throw in the towel. On the other hand, if you are connected to what drives you in your sport, you can find the fight in yourself to prove those people wrong.

Your Big Why can keep you going no matter what. Excuses disappear. Your potential becomes unleashed.

Knowing the reason you are committed to being a winner is a powerful resource that no one can take away from you. It is an unstoppable force that gives you meaning, strength and motivation. A deep inner drive propels you forward even when everyone else has given up.

When you connect to your Big Why, you become more dedicated to your sport, willing to make lifestyle changes, such as leaving people behind or modifying your social life.

Part of what kept me from transitioning from recreational to competitive rowing for more than a year was that I just couldn't see myself getting up at five in the morning. Eventually, however, my love for rowing became stronger than my resistance to the sacrifices I would have to make, and I became willing to make the commitment.

Some athletes naturally connect to their Big Why, but it's also possible to *decide* to do so. If you haven't already, will you make that decision now?

••An Exercise to Help You Connect with Your Big Why••

Think back to when you first started playing your sport. What did you love about it? How did it feel when you realized what you were capable of doing? Why did you decide to give everything you had for your sport?

Or, think of a time when you faced an obstacle in your sport. Perhaps someone was opposing you or criticizing you. Perhaps you were faced with an uncomfortable decision to make. What did you tell yourself to keep going despite the obstacle? What was your motivation to continue despite the odds?

On the lines below, write down three to five of those things. They are the makings of your Big Why.

Be honest, even if your motivation wasn't positive. Sometimes an athlete is driven not by a desire to win, but a desire to not lose. For example, a coach I did EFT with highly valued competing because his parents were very competitive themselves. He felt more loved when he won a competition and unloved when he didn't win. Competing wasn't about winning for him, but about not losing and not losing his parents' love. He had the goal to win and often did, but because his motivation was not losing, a struggle ensued, and he eventually quit playing.

If you're identifying with that story, it's good you're being honest. This is just the kind of subconscious material that this book can help you clear out. Once you do that, you can connect to something deeper, an internal motivator that can truly carry you to the fulfillment of your dreams.

MY BIG WHY

1. My 3-5 motivators were/are:

Need to provide for my family
Need to accomplish what my father did not.
Financial Means to flex my creativity
Financial means to be myself
To Desire to be extraordinary

2. Are the motivators positive or negative?

If one or more of your motivations is negative, it is possible to turn it around.

Here's a process, based on Byron Katie's *The Work,* for turning a negative motivation into a positive one:

• If your Big Why contains a negative statement, is it

true? If someone is playing "not to lose," an example of their negative statement might be, "I don't want to miss any passes."

• Is this the only way to look at the situation?

• When you think that negative statement what do you notice? Is there a certain sensation in your body? Or a change in energy?

• How would your focus be different if you didn't have that negative thought? Spend some time with this question. Let yourself imagine all the ways.

• Now, rephrase your statement to make it positive. For example instead of your goal being something you don't want to do, i.e., "Not miss any passes" you would make it a positive statement, i.e., "To catch passes thrown to me."

• Then make your positive goal as specific as possible. Modify "To catch passes thrown to me" to "To know where the ball will go and push myself to go for each pass thrown to me during practice and games."

Now, instead of a negative motivator, which encourages avoidance, you have a specific, positive motivator that will set you up for success. If you're used to motivating yourself in negative ways, positive motivators will be uncomfortable at first, but they will support you better over the length of your career.

The Gap

You know where you want to go and now you know *why* you want to get there. The question is: Why aren't you there? This is where your mental training truly begins.

The space between where you are now and where you would like to be is called "the gap."

All athletes driven toward excellence have a gap.

For instance, a dedicated golfer I worked with kept trying to lower his handicap on his own, but it just wasn't moving. The gap for him was the space between his 8.7 handicap and what he reached three months later, 5.7. My client was ahead of the game, so to speak, because he understood that the problem was mental not physical or technical.

Perhaps you want to play for the NFL or at Wimbledon or on the Senior Tour, but you keep missing the mark or you're just not there yet. That is the gap.

Once you commit to your goal, and recognize your gap, little steps to help you get there will begin to appear. Some of these stepping stones might have been there all along. You just never noticed them because your focus was elsewhere.

For example, a triathlete was preparing for her first Ironman competition. As you can imagine, that is a significant undertaking. She got nervous as soon as she signed up, realizing what she had committed to and needed reassurance of her capabilities.

The capability was in her, she just didn't see it at first. I helped her tap into the qualities and commitment level that had helped her to successfully rise up to a big goal she'd achieved earlier in her life. Those qualities were her stepping stones, revealing to her that she had the necessary capabilities to compete in the Ironman. Knowing it was within her, because she had already done it once, gave her the confidence to take it on.

How Do You Bridge the Gap?

The difference between the winners and everyone else boils down to one thing: how you choose to bridge the gap.

Your approach to the gap is determined by your beliefs, perceptions, prior experiences and support system. The most successful athletes take imperfect decisive action to close the gap. They continue making progress toward the next level of competition while correcting their course along the way.

The gap is not a problem, it's an opportunity.

Many athletes make the mistake of focusing on where they are now, what is right in front of them. Although the day-today training has to continue, you must remain focused on your goal, your vision. This is where your reason to excel comes in. Connecting to your Big Why will help you return your focus to your goal.

Before you can bridge the gap, you must first discover what it looks like for you. The following exercise will help you do that.

••An Exercise to Help You Discover and Cross the Gap••

Take a step back from where you are now. Think about your Big Why, about what motivates you to excel. Really drink it in.

Now, connect with the excitement and anticipation you feel as you imagine yourself as a winner, as you see the new records you are going to set and the life you will live. Tap into that feeling of being a winner.

How will your life be different once you reach your peak?

Write down five things about your life and the goals you will reach as a winner.

Where I want to be: *I can imagine . . . .*

1. *Buying expensive music equipment for Rowan*

2. *Walking through a public garden I funded*

3. *Offering my brother a job that pays a living wage.*

4. *Bidding high at a nonprofit fundraising event*

5. *Being flown somewhere for an important dinner arrangement.*

Now, consider your current performance. Where are you
now? Where aren't you getting the results that you want?
Under what circumstances do you get frustrated? What
challenges have affected your vision? How do you deal with
unforeseen circumstances? What are some of the thoughts
that go through your head?

Write down five of those things now.

Where I am:

1. _____

2. _____

3. _____

4. _____

5. _____

You now have a solid picture of your gap. You know where
you are and where you want to be.

The next step is to cross it.

It's important to have a tool for crossing the gap because
athletes can get stuck as they encounter it. They may give up,
and it doesn't have to be that way. With the proper tools and a
little support, you have what you need to get where you want
to go.

As I lead you through the various ways to cross the gap, I want
you to approach the process like a child. Here's what I mean.

When adults want to change a behavior they believe they

need to break an old habit first, whereas children just start something new.

Trying to break an old habit takes a lot of energy and keeps you focused on what you're not doing well. What you focus on expands, so not only are you wasting energy by trying to break a habit, you're focusing on the wrong thing.

When you approach change as a child, you're ready to try new things to find a better way. You move forward without any drag from the past.

Therefore, as you read the options below, think of them as helpful tools and new habits to adopt. Also, no tool is better than another. The one you are willing to use is the one that is right for you.

Tools for crossing the gap:

1. Reverse Engineering. My personal favorite approach for crossing the gap is to develop a plan from your future goal back to the present. This is called "reverse engineering." Along the way you create milestones. Those are the destinations of where you want to be by a specific date. Consider the steps you need to take to reach each milestone. This becomes your action plan.

Studies show that writing down your goal improves your chances for success. So let's do that right now. What would you like to accomplish by next year? Choose one goal. Then we will work the timeline backwards.

1. One year from now I would like to accomplish

_____

_____

_____

2. This is where I'll be in nine months

_____

_____

_____

3. My six-month milestone is

_____

_____

_____

4. My 90-day progress toward my goal is

_____

_____

_____

5. In 30 days I will be doing these things as I am working toward my one-year goal

_____

_____

_____

You now have an action plan for crossing the gap.

2. Be Creative. This process can be applied by the creative thinker as well as the cognitive planner. In this category many tools are available. Whatever your style, there is something for you.

One tool is a **vision board**, which generally is a collage of pictures cut out from magazines that represent where you want to be. It is a visual representation of your goal. It creates a picture in your mind, boosting the power of your written goals. Your vision board includes words and pictures that have meaning for you. When you look at it, you become inspired by what is possible.

Be sure to put onto your vision board the date by which you wish to accomplish your goal. Place your collage where you're likely to see it often so that you're inspired to keep crossing the gap. I keep mine in my bedroom by my dresser. I look at it first thing in the morning and right before I go to bed.

Other tools include **calendars, mind mapping** and **flow charts**.

By far the best **calendar** I have found for goal setting is Google calendars. It is user-friendly and can by accessed by any device with Internet access. Take the milestones you created in the above exercise and put them onto your Google calendar.

What makes Google calendar so easy is that different types of activities can be color coded for easy tracking. You can set different colors for physical vs. mental milestones. The activities to reach these milestones can also be added to your calendar with individualized colors as well. Maybe you are working on a goal to maintain positive mindset during competitions. By 90 days you want to maintain a positive focus for 75% of your event. That 90-day milestone could be color coded blue. Let's also say that twice a week you have committed to using visualization to reach your milestone. You will visualize yourself in difficult situations where you would normally be self-critical and instead you see yourself maintaining a positive perspective. (I'll show you how to do that in Chapter 6.) The days you use visualization are color coded green. Your physical goals might be orange and their corresponding activities in yellow.

To learn about **mind mapping**, check out the excellent video tutorial by its creator, Tony Buzan. As of this writing, it is available here: http://www.youtube.com/watch?v=MlabrWv25qQ.

Flow charts are a wonderful tool for linear thinkers who love to follow a step-by-step plan, see how the different steps are connected, and know about the important decisions along the way. As of this writing, this Web page gives a comprehensive explanation of flow charts for reaching a goal: http://www.mindtools.com/pages/article/newTMC_97.htm.

Whichever tool you choose, follow through. Keeping a plan in place to follow action steps and track progress increases your success rate. Consider trying two different tools to challenge both your right and left brain. You might be surprised by the results.

3. Choose a Buddy. If you realize you are getting off track with your training schedule or you're distracting yourself or making excuses, get an accountability buddy. Having another like-minded athlete whom you see or check in with on a regular basis is powerful. It helps you to maintain focus and keeps you on course.

Your buddy might be someone you train with or someone you talk with regularly. There are benefits to both types. If you're talking with your buddy, your check-ins should not be long conversations going over your training strategy. They should be brief five-minute talks, stating your intentions and goals for the day. They're designed to keep you accountable to your vision.

Hint: Whichever type of buddy you select, be strategic about your choice. Look for someone who is performing at a higher level than you are. This challenges you to improve. You will also observe how athletes at a higher level of proficiency think, train and perform. This will expand your awareness, setting you up for the next level of success.

In this chapter we've been working with your conscious mind, the thoughts you are aware of, to help you think like a winner. That's only part of the battle. In the next chapter, we're going to start talking about your subconscious mind, the part of you that is responsible for most of your actions and results.

Chapter 2

The Inner Struggle

A champion mindset is all about your attitude. It's about how you perceive something, and how you perceive something is determined by your experiences, the meaning you gave to your experiences, and the beliefs you created from those experiences.

Even though most people never consider questioning their beliefs, the good news is things can change. Beliefs, perceptions and even your subconscious can be altered. You can become conscious of what drives you, as well as your inner struggle, and you can change it all.

How Do You Perceive Setbacks?

When faced with a setback, are you the type to go with the flow, or to resist? Is your first response defeat, as though you'll never reach your goal? Do you see your setback as a failure?

Setbacks can actually set the stage for a breakthrough if you perceive them in a positive light, but too often we view them negatively, as failures. When you view them in a negative way, rather than as obstacles everyone faces or, preferably, as challenges, you become focused on what is not working well. Fear, doubt, worry and overwhelm set in. You start to experience what I call a "breakdown."

For instance, if you had a goal and you're not where you expected to be, you may find yourself using a lot of negative self-talk. If you're on a team and you're not up to par, you may wonder if you're worthy of practicing with your teammates. What if you're the star and you're not playing well? You might be concerned you're letting the other guys down, and become very hard on yourself. It's easy to slip into a negative mindset where you beat yourself up.

Whatever you focus on expands, so if you're focusing on where you are not yet and on the problems, it's hard to see solutions. You could be missing opportunities. Focusing on the problem also creates a struggle and a self-fulfilling prophecy. You begin to doubt yourself. Your confidence wanes.

Doubt is like a cancer. Once the seed of doubt gets planted in your mind, your ego, which actually wants to keep you where you are, recognizes the fear, feeds on it, and it expands. As I said, you break down.

How to Breakthrough

However, if you understand that a breakdown *always* occurs prior to a breakthrough, you can begin to turn the situation around. Not only does your perspective change, but your response changes as well. Instead of losing confidence, you begin to view the setback as just one more hurdle on your way to becoming a winner. Just take a moment and consider that. If you began training your mindset to switch from focusing on the problem to discovering solutions, your response would change. Instead of viewing situations as barriers, you would view them as challenges to overcome. And there is nothing like a good challenge to spark an athlete's competitive nature.

Too often, however, a breakdown will stop athletes because they are too identified with their ego.

When I refer to the ego, I'm talking about the part of us whose primary job is to keep us safe. Unfortunately, the ego tries to keep us safe by preventing us from actually taking risks and pushing ourselves. It can't discriminate between positive risk and negative risk, and views all risk as unsafe.

The doubts, fears and worries you experience are created by

the ego as it attempts to keep you where you are. Its perspective appears very, very real. It is the source of your resistance.

Among other things your ego is concerned with your image and how other people perceive you, external factors you are unable to control. Your ego is highly judgmental.

The more you move past your doubts and fear and continue to push yourself despite them, the less you are in need of your ego, and the last thing the ego wants is extinction. So, it raises the alarm even more. How? By causing you to experience more doubt, and bringing in guilt and shame.

Rather than trying to extinguish the ego and setting the stage for an internal battle to the death, aim, instead, for transformation. Become aware of your thoughts and emotions, and then change your response. Instead of believing you have to "do" something because you are feeling a certain way, just observe your emotions. See if you can acknowledge or name what you are feeling. You are much more complex than happy, sad, bored or angry. You don't need to do anything else. You don't have to try to change the feeling. Eventually it will change on its own.

I know that seems counter-intuitive because we are so conditioned to respond. But give it a try for one week and see how it is to note your emotions, whether fear, doubt or worry, but not to act on them. The choice is yours, act or react.

How to Transform the Ego Response

When I work with clients, we first identify their fears, doubts and worries, find out where they came from, what their purpose is, and then I look at how the client can take the underlying qualities of the ego response and use them in a positive way, in partnership.

For example, if you're experiencing a lot of fear and feel stuck, you may discover because of things that happened to you in childhood, your ego created a strong internal protector that's always on the lookout for danger. The problem is your protector can keep you from taking reasonable risks.

Risks come in all varieties. I am not suggesting you do something that would put you in a dangerous situation. I am encouraging you to step out of your comfort zone, challenge what you believe you are capable of doing. Stretching your perception about your capabilities leads to actually expanding your abilities.

Rather than fighting the ego, begin to think of it as a trailblazer. Give it a new job—the task of looking out for opportunities rather than threats or dangers.

Or, if you tend to be skeptical, always on the lookout for when you're going to get scammed, your distrustfulness and doubts may stop you from taking action. However, those same qualities also mean you're able to see down the road, to see the big picture. You're a strategist. The work, then, is to use those qualities in a positive way, as opposed to letting them stop you.

In truth, a setback or a breakdown is only a test of your commitment to your vision. View it as a challenge and reconnect to your Big Why. Remember your motivation for being a winner in the first place.

When you view setbacks as challenges, they don't knock you down. You just find a new way forward. You emerge victorious.

How Do You See the World?

Your life is like a movie. And the person sitting next to you or in the other room is viewing a very different movie.

The director of your movie is your perception. The way you experience anything and everything comes from how you perceive it. Is a setback a challenge or a catastrophe? It depends upon how you view it.

And the way you view it, as I said earlier, is determined by your experiences, the meaning you ascribed to them, and the beliefs you created from them.

What if setbacks are only an illusion, similar to the distractions that occur while competing? Not only can you change the way you view setbacks, but you can also change the lens of your perception. You can change the way you see *anything*. We're going to start with beliefs.

Beliefs Are Not Always Based on Logic

Beliefs are powerful. They determine whether you are going to be a star or not.

Consider the underdogs who became exceptional athletes despite the odds against them. They believed they were capable of great results, and they were. There are more athletes in history; however, who possessed the technical ability to be great, but didn't believe they could be. Their stories are rarely told.

Basically, a belief is the relationship between a thought and an emotion. As we grow up, situations and people influence us. Things happen in our life that have an emotional impact, and we create meaning around it and then form a belief based on the meaning.

There is a difference between a belief and reality. Beliefs are not always based upon facts or logic, although they feel very true. Beliefs, however, shape your reality.

Many of our beliefs were formed when we were very young, prior to age 7. This is an important fact. Before age 7 you are unable to distinguish between reality and fiction. Remember when you believed in the Tooth Fairy, the Easter Bunny and Santa Claus? Many of your beliefs were created in those early, formative years. Then they got tucked away into your subconscious.

As you grew up, you continued to create other beliefs, which also eventually went underground, becoming subconscious. You might not be aware of those beliefs, but they guide each decision you make and every action you take.

Over your life, you have formed a variety of beliefs about your performance, abilities and goals. Many have worked to your advantage. Other beliefs, however, prevent you from performing as well as you could. This is not good or bad; there is no judgment. Everyone possesses beliefs about their abilities.

Some of those beliefs are conscious and some are subconscious, or hidden. An example of a conscious belief would be: *I am a competitive rower.* A subconscious belief I had to contend with early on was, *I'm too short to win regattas.* Regattas are boat races (or boating competitions).

Subconscious beliefs are always more powerful than conscious beliefs, in part because they operate under the surface and we usually don't know they're there, but they still direct our actions. In fact if you have two opposing beliefs, one conscious and the other subconscious, the subconscious belief will always dominate.

How often do you see someone play great one game and then perform poorly the next? Something in that person's subconscious felt threatened about their success. It's as though they possess a speedometer on cruise control concerning their abilities. If they try to aim too high, or too low, the speedometer self-corrects to its set point.

Did that hit home? I bet it did. Most of us have something similar. I worked with a golfer who said she was a mid-70's golfer. Periodically her game would go to the low 70's, or even the high 60's, but not consistently. Her perception about being a mid-70's golfer was setting her average. We reset the cruise control on her speedometer to allow for a greater range, and she began having more games in the low 70's, which improved her average.

Conscious and subconscious beliefs are often in opposition to one another. Many subconscious beliefs were based on situations that don't exist anymore, and they were usually based on incomplete information to begin with. For instance, if your parents got divorced soon after you got in trouble for hitting the dog, you might conclude the divorce was your fault. You couldn't know the complexity of your parents' relationship; you only knew that you were "bad," and then Daddy left. You did not have all of the information, but in order to make sense of the situation, you attributed your own meaning to what happened. You completed a puzzle without all the pieces. You created a picture, but it wasn't accurate. Still, you formed a belief in your "badness," which moved into your subconscious and created problems for you later when it got activated or when it opposed a conscious belief.

Two opposing beliefs, especially a conscious and subconscious belief, create conflict and an inner struggle. For example, even if you say you are committed to being a top athlete, if you subconsciously believe you don't deserve it or don't want the attention, you'll hold yourself back, or worse yet, sabotage your success. Or you may become a perfectionist, slowing down your progress to avoid being judged for making a mistake.

Inner struggles are draining. Trying to think them through or tough them out will not help. The struggle is not based upon logic. It's energetic. It's like a water hose with a kink in it. No matter how much you turn on the faucet, the water will not flow. The kink holds back the water, creating pressure in the hose. However, once you take the kink out, the water flows freely.

When you develop an inner struggle because of two opposing beliefs, your energy has a kink in it, and progress becomes very difficult. Clear the kink and you begin to progress once more.

How to Clear the Kink
My client Allan was a nationally-ranked junior tennis player, who was going into his first season competing at the national level.

He was very happy about being nationally ranked, but the road there was not easy for him. Although he has great technical abilities, something was missing from his game. He told me he was not getting the results he expected. He talked about the challenges to get there, how tough the competition was at his level and how he was fighting to move up in position.

His language was all about struggle, which told me he had an internal struggle, a collision between conscious and subconscious beliefs.

When I pointed this out to him, he was willing to explore his hidden beliefs and make any connections between those beliefs and his current results.

After some discussion, he admitted tennis wasn't fun for him anymore. Playing at the national level was hard work. He practiced long hours, his parents were always talking about the sacrifices they were making to support his tennis game, and as he progressed in rankings, he felt the pressure of more and more being expected from him.

Like a lot of athletes, he had the common belief that he needed to tough it out. Yes, that is one way to move past a performance obstacle. It is not, however, the easiest way nor is it going to earn the quickest, long-lasting results.

It certainly wasn't working for Allan.

Allan's solution was much simpler. Rather than tough it out, I suggested he put into action a new belief that competitive tennis could be fun. I suggested he create rest periods so he would be more relaxed while playing, and also find ways to bring the fun back into his game. I told him if he was having fun and not using the results as a measure of his success he would play better and be more focused.

He agreed to try out some of the suggestions, with the goal of having fun during practice and tournaments. To really make this work, however, his parents needed to be aware of the plan. They agreed to stop talking about the sacrifices they were making to support him and vowed to be more encouraging.

With his new belief that competitive tennis could be fun and the support from his parents, Allan's performance improved significantly and he became excited about his game.

Some beliefs are easily changed on your own once you recognize them. Others are more challenging. They can change, but are more deeply rooted. Once you are genuinely ready to replace your belief with something new and relevant, however, it will happen. Change is possible.

••An Exercise to Clear the Kink••

To begin to clear your own kink caused by conflicting beliefs, try the same three-prong approach I used with Allan:

1. Uncover the hidden beliefs affecting your performance.

First, examine your resistance. Where are you not excelling as expected? When do you hold yourself back? When do make excuses, blame others or feel fear? In those situations, it's likely you are experiencing conflicting beliefs. Choose one situation and try to find the belief that is informing your action or inaction. (To do this, you might need the assistance of a sports psychologist or coach.)

2. Discover the relationship between the belief and the consequences it is having on your performance. The easiest way to do this is to become aware of the thoughts you are having during your performance. How do those thoughts influence your actions? After your competition, write down where you experienced flow and what was occurring. Also note when you felt like it was difficult to remain focused and what was going on then.

3. Regain control by exploring alternative beliefs better suited for your current reality, and put those beliefs into action. The ideal time to do this is after your competition when you have time to reflect on your performance.

If you had difficulty with this exercise, don't despair. Sometimes, it takes a trained professional to help you clear the obstacles to success. And, similar to coaching, you will transform the obstacles at a faster pace working with someone else than you will on your own.

The Power of Your Story

The beliefs you have feel true, but, as I've said, they are creations of your experiences. They stem from your interpretation of the things that happen to you and the story you tell yourself in order to make sense of the event.

We all have a story, and each of our stories is unique. Our stories can inspire us or hold us back. But, as I'll show you shortly, even the ones that hold us back can be transformed.

One of my clients, Tom, a track and field competitor, is preparing for the Olympics. During a session, we were talking about his childhood, when he was chunky and awkward. All the neighborhood kids, including him and his sister, used to get together and play kickball in the field.

Tom was one of the younger kids in the neighborhood and usually one of the last kids picked for the teams. He told me that nobody wanted him because his weight slowed him down. They teased him about his size, chanting a mean sing-song rhyme. Instead of defending him, his sister sang along.

Tom endured this treatment for a long time, and it eroded his confidence. When you hear something repeatedly, you begin to believe it. When Tom came to me he admitted he did not like being the center of attention. He would rather hide. This posed a problem for Tom. When he was competing and the stands were filled with spectators, he experienced anxiety. You can imagine how a reluctance to be the center of attention would create an inner struggle and hold him back.

How We Changed Tom's Story to Match His Goals

Most people never stop to examine their beliefs, to see if they ought to be updated. Then when something occurs in the present to activate one of those subconscious beliefs you formed when you were a child, you respond or react to it like a child without even realizing it.

It's as though your five-year-old self steps up and starts driving the bus. Now, five-year-olds do not have the skill set or maturity to drive responsibly—you don't want them directing your responses. Yet, when a triggering event occurs, we all can respond from a very old place, especially when caught off guard. That's why you see athletes having tantrums during a game.

Luckily, humans are extremely adaptable. Our brain has plasticity. That's one of the reasons we have survived as a species. We are flexible, evolving beings. And we can use our innate adaptability in order to change our future or even our past.

Just like you can change how you view setbacks, you can change how you view your memories. When you do that, you don't have to forget the memory, you just alter how you look at it and the way it affects you. Ideally the memory loses its charge, its emotional intensity. Once that is gone, you are free to create a new response to a situation that previously would have triggered a reactive response.

Rather than perceiving the event the way the five-year-old viewed it and believing the story that he or she created, you get to rewrite the story and perceive the event from an adult's point of view.

This impacts your training, your competition and your life.

During only one session, we changed Tom's story around his childhood experience of the kickball games. Using EFT and visualization, which I'll explain in detail in Chapter 6, we shifted his focus from the negative, being teased for his weight, to the positive.

Using visualization, I took Tom back to a kickball game and had him see himself there as the young boy he was and also as the man he is today.

Most of the emotional charge around that incident was anger at his sister for not defending him, so while I did the EFT, I invited him to say all the things to her that he had wanted to say for two decades. This caused a big emotional release for him.

Then, we created a new mind movie, altering the memory to be positive, by reframing his after-school days playing kickball as a major contributor to his vow to be the best. We transformed a lifelong negative memory into a strong motivator for becoming an elite track and field competitor. By doing so, he reconnected to his personal commitment to becoming strong and athletic.

Instead of being a negative memory of being teased, which held him back, he now views his years of kickball as his impetus to excellence.

In addition, we developed a powerful visualization that he can now tap into of being the winner at competitions.

Changing Tom's story significantly boosted his confidence during competitions. He now knows how to remain focused, dismissing things that would have previously distracted him. After one session his performance improved significantly without any additional physical training.

Retool Your Inner Critic

A relentless inner critic can also cause a kink that will prevent you from thinking like a winner.

Most top athletes have very high standards for themselves. They feel they never perform to their best potential, there's always something they could do to push their limit a bit more. Those thoughts of always wanting to do more and never being satisfied can, and do, motivate a person to try harder, to work harder.

At a certain point, however, self-criticism can backfire. Those thoughts of never doing well enough are very negative, and negativity slows down progress.

For instance, when you're critical, you tend to second-guess everything you do and you may hold back, fearful of making a mistake and being criticized again, if only by yourself. Also, when you are giving so much energy to what you are not doing well, it drains you. It's exhausting.

Change is also difficult when you are focusing on what you don't want to do, what is not working for you and what you are not doing well. When you keep looking behind you, you are going against the flow, hindering your success. Remember, whatever you focus on expands. By thinking negative thoughts, you will find evidence to support your reality.

This is like rafting upstream on a river. By going against the current, you spend a lot of energy resisting the river's natural flow. It is tiring and exhausting. For the amount of effort you're exerting, you have little gain in return. On the other hand, if you turn your raft around to go downstream with the natural current of the river, your raft flows easily with little effort.

In the same way, when you turn your attention toward what *is* working, what you are doing well and where your performance is improving, you're looking forward. You're positive and hopeful, excited by what's possible. Your raft is now going downstream, aided by the current. You begin taking steps toward reaching your peak performance.

It is important, however, to be aware of the messages your critical voice is telling you. If you're not aware of them, you can't change the situation. Some athletes aren't aware, so they're attacked and don't even know it. As a result they may act out, underachieve, or be unpredictable or moody.

How You Can Become Aware (if You're Not)

If you aren't aware of the self-critical voice in your head, it is possible to hear it. Just as you keep logs on your performance, keep logs or journals on the thoughts you have that put you into the zone, as well as the thoughts that create distraction for you. You might be surprised to find that when you are in the zone, your mind is clear, free of all thought.

If you begin to log your thoughts, then you're starting to bring something that was subconscious up to the surface. And once you are aware of those hidden thoughts, you can begin to change the situation.

Next, it is important to understand how those negative thoughts affect your performance. When you're doing your log, record the connection between each thought or thoughts and a result. For instance, let's say you're a golfer and you recall that you were beating yourself up for missing the last hole and, as a result, you lost focus.

Once you become aware of the self-critical messages, the trick is to not believe them. They sound justified, but they're not.

Those messages originally came from someone else. You might have heard them from a parent or a teacher. Most likely you heard them from someone you really wanted praise from, but never got. You can choose to transform your inner critic, and as you do, you're freeing yourself of the negative drag on your performance.

••An Exercise to Sidestep Your Inner Critic••

Here are six steps for transforming your relationship with the inner critic:

1. First, understand that the inner critic is fearful. Fearful thoughts can easily take on a life of their own, causing a complete halt of any progress if ignored. What are the fears that keep you stuck?

2. You get to choose how you view your progress and performance. Despite what your inner critic says, you don't have to focus on the negative, on what you're not doing well, in order to excel. Remember, to do so is like rafting upstream. Create a strengths-based approach, finding the positive activities that help you improve.

3. It feels as though the inner critic is part of you, but it is not. Having awareness of this will help you separate

from the critical voice. Where did the critical thoughts originate? If you hear them, do you recognize the voice?

4. Once you recognize you have a choice to release the inner critic, you have created your opportunity for change. Choose not to believe the voice anymore.

5. Your goal is not to annihilate the voice. Your goal is to make it irrelevant. Do that by shifting your focus to the positive. Acknowledge the activities you are doing well. Become aware of your strengths. Choose the next step toward your vision. Think about your goals.

6. Notice the results. As you begin changing your perception and thinking like a winner, the resistance to your excellence collapses, and you will start to see improvement in your performance. In addition, you will have a much-improved state of mind.

To be a winner, you have to think like a winner, see yourself as a winner, and act like a winner. Each of these steps is more involved than it seems on the surface.

Like with Tom, it may require a willingness to delve into memories you wish you could forget. The good news is once you do, you're free. You will no longer have a drag on your performance. You'll have fewer distractions affecting your focus, and your performance will certainly improve.

You can choose to release yourself from the struggle, your resistance and your inner critic. Thinking like a winner changes your brain chemistry, setting the stage for an upward spiral and a breakthrough in performance.

I know that's what you want. So let's continue.

Chapter 3

Champions Think Outside the Box

When athletes are competing in a team sport or working with a coach, there is a usual and customary way to train that, for the most part, works for the average player. However, when athletes get truly connected to their vision and desire to be the best they possibly can be, they start looking for other things they could be doing to help them reach their goal.

The really motivated athletes go the extra mile, pushing themselves in ways most athletes don't. For example, Olympic Gold Medal winner Lindsey Vonn trains regardless of the conditions. She is out there skiing when it's sleeting or raining or, even, during blizzards.

Instead of waiting for someone to tell them what to do, motivated athletes take a proactive role in their training, including seeking training in areas they might not be getting from their own coach.

A client of mine, who is a hammer thrower, realizes he has a tendency to be too much in his head. While preparing for the U.S. National's Track and Field Competition, he wasn't getting specific help with this from his coach, so I asked him who threw the way he would like to throw, which was connecting with the hammer as if it were an extension of himself.

It turned out he had a role model who threw more rhythmically and naturally, so he reached out to this person, traveled to another city and trained with him for a week.

Instead of just complaining about his coach and being frustrated, he took a proactive role and got the training he needed.

Be Open to Unusual Opportunities

Success-minded athletes look for opportunities to help them reach their goals, and those opportunities might not be usual and customary.

In fact, to be a highly successful winning athlete *requires* out-of-the-box thinking and a more creative approach.

In-the-box, traditional training is what everybody is doing. In this model, you go with the flow, don't question things, and accept the feedback you're getting as fact as opposed to considering if there might be a better way. If your intention is to remain average then this approach will serve its purpose. Athletes who desire continued improvement ought to modify traditional practices, creating an individualized training approach. Notice if there are particular parts of your training program where you get exceptional results. If so, consider discussing with your coach the modification of your training program to maximize the components where you receive the best results. Personal excellence requires psychological along with physical commitment.

If you want to be a top athlete, you have to rise above the rest. If you just do what everybody is doing, you're going to get the same results they are. If you want different results, you have to train differently.

Below, are a few ways to begin.

How to Break Out of the Box

1. Push the edge. You do have to learn the rules first, but once you understand them, you can break them, go beyond the theory and push the edge. Athletes who are geared for success are compelled to look for new ways forward. They want to find the challenge of seeing how far they can go.

2. Be open to inspiration no matter where it originates. Like it did for my hammer thrower client, your inspiration might come from a role model in your own sport or it might come from a different sport. You may take a concept from ice hockey and apply it to gymnastics.

I do this all the time when I apply business and success concepts to athletics, which, in fact, transfer very well. For example, the three components necessary for success are the same: having a vision of what you want to be, having the motivation to keep going and stay connected to your vision even when obstacles arise, and taking action to continue moving toward your vision.

Similarly, you might study highly successful people in other sports to determine if what they did to achieve their success will transfer to your sport.

Inspiration is all around you. You have only to be open to it.

3. View failure differently. You have to stop seeing failure as negative. Instead, view it as a learning opportunity that highlights the areas that need further strengthening or shows you where a new approach might be necessary to reach your desired results.

4. Connect with athletes who are like-minded. If you are a highly-driven athlete, it's important to connect with other highly-driven athletes, in or outside of your sport, because they know things you don't know yet, and vice versa. Like the adage 1+1=3, the two of you coming together form a third consciousness, out of which can develop new ideas as well as inspiration.

5. Take personal responsibility. Instead of relying upon someone to tell you what to do and then just following the person's direction, take ownership of your vision and goal. Ask questions or seek information to help you get where you want to go.

If your current coach is only able to take you to a particular point in your career, but no further, look for the person who can stretch you to reach your goal.

Or, if your current coach is not the best match for you—perhaps he or she is very high-strung or overly negative—and you're in a position to choose your coach, find the person who is going to support you in the way that works best for you.

However, if you *can't* choose or change your coach, don't complain about it or throw in the towel. Find someone else who is able to give you the support you need. Maybe the assistant coach's temperament is better suited for you.

But before you give up on your first coach, communicate your needs to him or her—if your coach is approachable. I know, some aren't, but some are, if you approach them with respect. Take the initiative to educate your coach about your best learning style.

You have yet another option. If you don't like the way your coach communicates with you, try to look past the negativity and really understand the coach's intention. Your coach wants you to do well, because when you do well, he or she looks good.

So learn how to perceive differently what your coach or, even your teammates, are saying.

A lot of times, you can change your perception, and your experience, simply by not taking it so personally, even though it feels personal.

You can make a decision to not get upset anymore.

6. Look for the Purple Cow. As Seth Godin wrote in his book *The Purple Cow,* when you're driving along the highway and you see all the black and white cows, you don't really take any notice because they blend in with the expected scenery. However, if all of a sudden you see a purple cow, you're going to stop, pull your car over and really look at the cow because it's different.

If you're looking to break a record, traditional coaching is not going to get you there. You need to look for a different approach. You need to look for the purple cow.

A current example, as of this writing, is Novak Djokovic, the

Serbian tennis player, who's positioning himself to become the world champion tennis player.

Djokovic was not expected to be in this position, but he had a couple of wins and started to feel more confident. He brought his extra confidence into his practices and, as a result, started having better practices and getting more out of them. He also began to manage his emotions more effectively. How he was showing up shifted.

Along with his changed mindset and growing self-confidence, he dedicated his training to fitness, quickness and consistency to develop a more aggressive game on the court. The combination of mindset and a more aggressive physical training program became a winning combination for him. He found the purple cow. He mastered his inner power and reconnected to his motivation to win. He began taking more risks—and started beating people who had been beating him for years.

Yes, other elite athletes have successfully applied mindset and training for winning results. This combination, however, was new to Djokovic. Suddenly, he came upon a new formula and everything shifted. He learned how to get out of the struggle.

What separates Djokovic from the others is his playful personality. Basically, he is a ham, joking and playing along with his fans, impersonating others. His sense of fun, along with his dedicated approach to tennis keeps him grounded. Humor is a great stress reducer, which helps you keep everything in perspective.

As I've said, winning is 90% mindset. Players stepping onto the court or into the field with confidence, believing in their ability to win, play in a different manner than players who are solely thinking about what place they will finish.

Vision-Based, Out-of-the-Box Training

Don't misunderstand me. There are definitely aspects of traditional training you ought to be doing because they've been proven to work. My point is, don't stop there. Look for opportunities that will help you reach your vision, regardless of where those opportunities come from.

At first, they might not appear to make sense or might seem inconvenient, but be receptive to them because, in the long run, they're going to help you get where you want to go at a quicker pace.

A powerful example of out-of-the-box training occured in Indonesia. From 1977 to 2001, the country excelled in badminton, and before championship matches, during practices, they offered free tickets to residents to come and fill the stands to give the players the sense of being in a serious competition.

As European players began appearing in international tournaments, they created a new challenge for the Indonesians because the Europeans were taller. What did the Indonesians do? They rebuilt their courts to compensate for the difference in height. On the new courts, ranked Indonesian players got used to playing someone who is taller.

Indonesia's vision-based training paid off and they started to win again.

In addition, higher-ranked Indonesian players help train the beginners, who are just starting to prepare for the Olympics. This helps both groups. Younger players get used to practicing with people with a lot of experience, and the higher ranked players gain the reinforcement of the concepts and principles that comes from teaching what you know.

In another example, closer to home, I was working with a gymnastics team, and one of the gymnasts told me she does great during practice on the beam exercise, but during competitions the floor exercise music and people clapping for other events breaks her concentration and throws off her timing.

My solution was having her teammates make a lot of noise during practice, trying to distract her, so she could learn how to tune them out and stay focused. In her next state championship competition, she easily tuned out the distracting noise to focus on her performance. With her increased concentration she was able to stick her back flips.

Learn to Love What Challenges You Today

I encourage you to do the same. Recreate the circumstances of your biggest challenge and train under those circumstances in order to learn how to effectively overcome your challenge.

For example, some athletes don't like competing outdoors during a cold rain or in windy conditions because the weather affects performance. For those athletes, inclement weather is going to be very frustrating. They'll be very aware of the conditions and how that affects the event area, and that will drain their energy and focus. Instead of being focused on performance, they'll become distracted by the elements, which are factors beyond their control.

If I've just described you, and you don't like competing when it's drizzling or raining, I'm saying practice during those conditions, so you can learn how to remain focused regardless of the weather, and even find out how to love those conditions.

If you can learn to love what you've always hated or avoided, you're going to have a very different outlook. Inclement weather will be just another way to challenge yourself. Or you might be neutral. You'll think, *Okay, these are not the conditions that I expected, but hey, I'm here. I'm going to do my best.* And that will have a very different effect on your energy level and performance than if you got upset, frustrated, and angry about something that's completely out of your control.

If you think it's not possible to learn to love something you hate now, let me tell you, it is. For six years, I avoided rowing in a single. As the name implies, a single is a boat with one rower. While I enjoyed the challenging physical workout, I missed the camaraderie of sharing the practice with others in the same boat. Rowing in a boat by myself felt like punishment. I knew I had to get past my aversion, so I tackled the issue and *made* myself row in a single. I pushed past my resistance and was surprised to discover I actually enjoyed it.

Being alone in a boat offers a different focus than in a group. Training side by side with other singles challenges me. We end up pushing each other. Time flies by. Being comfortable in any size boat makes me more versatile. And, now, I actually prefer to row in a single most days of the week.

To make a similar shift for yourself, understand that you're not given any challenges you are unable to overcome. If you connect with your vision and you can see yourself having reached your goal, then the way for you to attain it is always available to you.

You will have to move outside of your comfort zone, and, going back to Chapter 2, reframe any beliefs holding you back. For instance, I believed I couldn't have fun rowing by myself, but once I gave it a chance, I saw that wasn't so.

The action didn't change. I still was rowing alone. But how I perceived the action changed, and that changed everything.

Part Two

See Yourself as
a Winner Now

Chapter 4

Where is Your Focus?

What matters is where you want to go.
Focus in the right direction!
—Donald Trump

You Are a Star

Everything you need in order to win is available to you right now. All you need to do for your dream to become a reality is to believe it is possible, and then take action when the opportunities appear. It really is that simple.

Now this does not mean all you have to do is think about something and it will happen. And it doesn't mean you won't face setbacks along the way. What it does mean is you need to recognize and say "yes" to the opportunities that are available to you right now.

For instance, what could you be doing to improve your performance? Would you benefit by working with a speed, strength or jump coach? Could you enhance your nutrition or self-care? Explore different ways to train?

Star athletes are committed to the game. They adopt a no-excuses approach to winning. Commit now to be at the top of your game. Look for the next step that can take you to your goal, then follow through, take action.

The Brick Wall

Along the way to your goal, you will be tested to see how committed you are to excellence. Remember what I said about setbacks? Napoleon Hill, author of *Think and Grow Rich*, called them the "sly guises of opportunity." They appear unfortunate, but they're not. These moments separate the winners from the rest.

For example, as you progress in your events, moving up in rankings, eventually you're going to plateau and your progress will come to a halt. You'll experience a slump. A setback. You'll hit a brick wall.

Most athletes respond to a brick wall by digging in, trying harder, doing whatever they can to get past it. As competitive people, when confronted with the fight, flight, or freeze response, athletes want to fight. White knuckling and working through it feels like the natural response.

The problem is trying to put more muscle into the situation actually creates more of a struggle, because you're getting very focused on what's not going well, which can dig you in deeper. It's like the quicksand analogy, where if you step into quicksand, the more you fight and struggle, the quicker you're going to sink. The best response to quicksand is to relax, which actually buys you time to look around for the opportunity to get yourself out.

The same is true when you're in a slump or plateau. Rather than struggling and digging yourself in deeper, take some time to assess the situation. View the brick wall as a test to see how committed you are to your vision. Also, realize a plateau is just an indication of your body rearranging itself as it prepares to take you to the next level of performance. It appears at first to be a setback, but it's not. Instead, a shift is happening in your body. Energy is being used to successfully prepare you for the next level of performance.

It's similar to the way you harness your energy right before a race, game or competition. You're waiting for the event to start and you're anticipating your turn. Think about the physical and mental preparation right before you "go," the way you're gathering your energy so you can burst into action.

Your slump or setback is the same. Transition periods *require* larger amounts of focused energy to allow you to successfully leap from where you are now to where you want to be. In truth, you are doing this all the time, but when it appears unexpectedly it catches you off guard and throws you off balance.

Instead of getting discouraged, keep your faith and remain connected to your vision of what you're capable of doing. Continue to work on your technique, your strength, whatever you need to do, but remain confident that you will continue to improve.

Star Athletes Value Progress and Learning

When star athletes smack into a brick wall they keep their focus on where they want to go and continue to take the necessary steps to regain momentum. They look for any opportunity to get where they want to go. Their vision is clear and they are committed to taking quick, decisive action while maintaining their focus on their goal.

They are also more committed to progress than perfection. This is important, and it's a departure from traditional thought. More often than not athletes are concerned about how they look, avoiding mistakes at all costs. Well, what if avoiding mistakes turned out to be costly? What if it cost priceless experience? Would you become less concerned with appearances and more committed to making the attempts?

If a star athlete's action is not perfect, he or she will make adjustments along the way. A champion mindset puts the ego aside and values experience over appearance. Failure is not an option. Instead, the champion views mistakes as learning opportunities, and corrections and adjustments as part of the path to excellence.

Athletes who have hit a brick wall are weighted down in some capacity. Something old needs to be "let go" in order to move forward. They're like the pilot of a hot air balloon who wants the balloon to go higher, to a new altitude. To achieve that new height, the balloon needs to lighten its load. Perhaps you need to do the same. What do you need to let go?

When you look at the stats, top athletes actually have more setbacks than the rest. They also put more time into their training than everyone else, stretching themselves, testing new techniques and pushing toward the edge. These athletes are set on what they believe is possible, even when others have doubt. "No" is not an acceptable answer for champions. Instead of stating they can't do something, they are wondering how they can make it happen.

For example, when basketball great Michael Jordan was a sophomore in high school he was not chosen to be on the varsity team because he was not tall enough. Another player, who was also a sophomore, got a place on the varsity team. Although he was not as good as Michael, he was taller. This got Michael so angry he became even more motivated to become great.

Michael believed in what he was capable of doing, and he stuck with it, and his results speak for themselves.

If you can adopt a similar paradigm shift it will begin to change your attitude and focus. It will get you ready for the breakthrough.

How to Get Beyond the Brick Wall

Getting beyond the brick wall does not mean you have to do it alone. You may need to find someone to help you make your leap to your next level of performance. Star athletes have a lot of support: coaches, trainers and buddies. The people who support you the most, believing in your ability to win and sharing your vision of excellence, want to help you get beyond the brick wall. They want you to succeed. They cannot do your work, but they continue to believe in you as you take the next step. They mirror your ability to win.

Like with Michael Jordan, your commitment to your vision of what is possible propels you forward. Success comes from taking inspired action, seeing an opportunity and grabbing it. Success is a race against time on several dimensions. If you are working toward a specific goal, realize that the goal has also been seeded in other determined athletes. Many different athletes are dedicating their time, energy and efforts to the very same outcome. So what one thing is necessary to declare the winner? The answer is continued inspired action. The record holder takes inspired action toward his or her goal, and they take quick, decisive action. Implementing with speed separates the top performers from the rest.

Where Do Your Eyes Land?

When you're competing, a myriad of external distractions in your environment can disrupt your focus. These include the weather conditions, very loud spectators, a teammate who's getting on your nerves. You could have some type of equipment malfunction, such as an oar breaking during a regatta, a tire going flat while cycling, your goggles coming off when you dive into the water, or the basketball hoop not being perfectly placed and, therefore, affecting your throws.

You can also experience internal distractions, which are the thoughts and emotions you have in response to external distractions, as well as any internal dialogue and thoughts about previous competitions where you did not perform your best. You could be looking at your opponents and perceiving them to be bigger, stronger or more confident than you are.

These distractions shift your focus away from your game and negatively affect your performance. Sizing up the competition impacts confidence. When you focus on the past, you may experience depression. If you're focusing on something you're afraid will happen, you'll feel anxiety. Negative thoughts drain energy and cause self-doubt. Your inner critic slows you down.

Recently I was talking with an infielder who'd been playing for years. He knew what it felt like to be in the zone and what he was capable of, but for whatever reason, he couldn't catch a ball for anything.

He didn't understand why he was playing poorly, and the tricks he knew to help him get centered and focused weren't working. He was struggling, digging himself in, and the situation was getting worse. His concentration was off and his confidence was falling. For the whole day before a game, he would be concerned about his performance rather than being present with his family, which was affecting their relationship. The situation was also affecting the rest of his training and his play. He should have been the top batter but, instead, was at the bottom of the batting lineup. He was in a breakdown and knew he needed help.

If we worked together, I would discover why he was so distracted, and then help him get out of the struggle. His new insight would help to improve his game. I would also teach him the various mindset and focus techniques (visualization, EFT, and keywords) I'll be sharing with you in this book.

Once the block has been identified and cleared, a void is created. This is why it is so important to replace something old with something new. Replace the negative with a positive.

I took this approach with a golfing client who came to me after being unable to shake the impact of a particular hole where it took her 14 strokes to sink her ball. She was beating herself up about her performance, and it was affecting her confidence. Because she tends to be a perfectionist, she was looking at the hole as a failure and, therefore, the incident was weakening her golf game and working against her.

I encouraged her to turn the situation around by viewing it as an opportunity to understand what was affecting her concentration in the first place, and then use the information to do something differently and, thus, strengthen her overall game.

This was also the approach the young golfer Rory McIlroy took when he played the Master's in Augusta, Georgia, in April of 2011. He was strongly positioned to win and entered the fourth game of the series with a four-stroke lead. If he had won the famous Green Jacket, at 22, he would have been the second youngest golfer in history to do so.

But after his tee shot on the 10th hole ricocheted off a tree and settled out-of-bounds, his focus unraveled. It took him a long time to get his ball back onto the green, and his composure was shaken. He was unable to leave his last shot behind and focus on his current shot. The domino effect set in, quickly erasing his four-shot lead.

Rather than beat himself up for playing poorly, however, he chose to look at the situation as an opportunity that could eventually improve his game. He realized his rankings in the tournament plus his significant lead had caused some extra tension for him. He had been more focused on his placement than on keeping his head in the game and on the shot right in front of him. By not winning the Green Jacket he learned a valuable lesson and is unlikely to have the same experience in the future.

Where is Your Focus?

If you have a disappointing performance, like the infielder, are you unable to get past it? Do your thoughts turn to bad calls made by the referee or unfavorable conditions? Are you easily distracted? Do you see a pattern here? All these thoughts are based upon things you cannot control. You are spinning your wheels, wasting your most valuable asset—your energy—on something you have absolutely no control over.

It's vital to learn how to hone your focus and minimize the impact of distractions. To do so, become aware of what your brain perceives as its object. For instance, do you tend to look at the target you want to hit in your sport or the outcome you are avoiding? If it's the latter, the simple act of placing your focus on the target is your important first step.

The next step is to learn to focus on what you want.

Focus Where You Want to Go

Thoughts, vision and results are inter-connected. If you believe something will happen, you begin to look for cues to affirm your belief. This creates conditions that eventually will produce an outcome supporting your belief. Simply put, if you believe something is true, it is. Everything will align itself to prove you are right.

Your mindset is powerful. It can boost you up or bring you down.

I've told you one of my favorite things to do is to row around the lake near my house. I do this six days a week, while focusing on conditioning and training to prepare me for race day.

Over the years I've learned about the value of practice, practice and more practice. Due to my commitment to improving my technique, I've experienced some amazing outcomes.

Before a regatta in July of 2010, I was in two races, one with my doubles partner, and the other in an eight-person boat. The doubles race was my main event. I knew who my competition was. This is where my mindset and focus became crucial.

My partner, Michele, and I are both petite lightweights. As I've said, I'm 4'11" and I was 48 at the time. Michele was 60 and only 5'3". My competitors were physically stronger, a decade younger, and a foot taller than me.

You get the picture. How could we possibly compete against women who held such a physical advantage?

Here's how. Instead of being intimidated by their size, youth and strength, we stayed focused on *our* advantage, which was technical skills and time in the boat together, which meant excellent rhythm. In order to beat them in the heat, we knew we needed to win with technique, and we were determined to do so.

The first heat in the double was a 1000-meter race, which is over in less than five minutes. We came in second, only a couple of seconds behind the winner, which put us in a final heat against the first-place boat.

The second heat was a Henley, a 2000-meter race. Before the heat, Michele and I discussed our race plan and corrected aspects of our performance that hadn't gone well the first time.

We had an excellent start, stuck with our plan, and rowed for our life. We put everything into our race and maintained our lead the entire time, finishing first by 1 second! We were so excited.

No one comparing us to our competitors would have put their bets on us. But *we* knew we had the technical and experience advantage, so we felt confident about the event. Our confidence, focus and determination gave us the win.

What it all boils down to is if you think you can do something, you can. If you believe you can't, you can't.

A bowling client of mine learned this lesson recently. During the first game of a tournament, he bowled under 200. In the past, this less-than-ideal score would have haunted him the rest of the night.

Instead, rather than letting his score worry him and affect his bowling, he decided to shake it off, using several techniques I had taught him to regain focus and keep it laser sharp.

His result? What began as a disappointing game turned into a milestone. He bowled a perfect 300 that night!

His bowling 300 was similar to a runner breaking the 4-minute mile. He was 62 and had been trying to bowl a perfect game for decades. Several times he had come close but something always prevented him from breaking the barrier.

He now knows what was once impossible is possible. He has increased confidence about his abilities and gets more respect from his teammates.

If he hadn't had the mindset techniques, he likely would have allowed his first game to throw off the rest of his evening. He would have had a lot of negative inner dialogue and would have continued to chase his dream of a perfect game, wondering if he could ever reach his goal.

Instead, he kept his focus on the result he wanted and bowled his best game ever.

Frame What You Want in Positive Terms

Whatever you focus on expands, so if you're focusing on something you don't want to do, or are worried about, then that very thing is likely to happen. This happens because subconsciously you're giving your brain messages to be attuned to the very action you don't want to have happen.

The brain operates through images. It doesn't have an image for the word "no" or "not." So when you think about what you *don't* want to happen; for instance, you think you "do not want to go out of bounds," the brain focuses on the noun and the verb, so it hears that you "want to go out of bounds."

This explains a lot, doesn't it? Just think about the golfer who is obsessing about the sand trap at the 5th hole, hoping his ball does not go there this time. Sure enough, he gets to the hole and 8 out of 10 times his ball lands in the sand trap. Or what about the star basketball player who messes up the free throw from the foul line over and over again. He is tuning into all of his past misses, hoping it does not happen this time, but quite likely it does. He can't figure out why that always happens. It happens because his brain wants to make him happy and does so by giving him what he's focusing upon.

Most of us are wired to focus on the negative, which has been reinforced again and again since we were babies: *Don't do this. Don't touch that. Don't cross the street without looking both ways.* We don't even realize we're focusing on a goal or an objective from a negative point of view.

Another factor at play is that memory is reinforced by the amount of emotion we attribute to an experience. When we're focusing on not going out of bounds, and the ball goes out of bounds, we get frustrated and angry and critical of ourselves. All of those emotions reinforce the memory.

In a psychology class, I was told that a medieval village used strong emotion to pass down its oral history. On important days they wanted recorded, they would choose a young child and tell the child to really pay attention to everything that happened in the village that day. At the end of the day, they would take the child, who couldn't swim, and throw him into the water. They knew the fear he experienced would seal in his memories and the events of the day.

So the question is: what memories are you sealing in? Are you making sure you always remember your successes? Or, are you perpetuating your disappointments?

If you're like most people, you're doing more of the latter, but it is possible to create a new habit.

It's possible to begin focusing on the result you would like to have. Rather than saying you don't want the ball to go out of bounds, focus on what you do want to happen. If what you want is to hit the ball 250 yards down the middle, envision yourself doing so before taking your practice swings. If you want to increase your percentage of free throws, see yourself in your mind's eye sinking them smoothly every time. Seeing yourself doing something is called visualization, a powerful tool I'll explore in depth in Chapter 6.

•• An Exercise to Train Your Inner Focus ••

With a crystal-clear inner focus, distractions lose their power to throw you off course, and you can perform consistently under any and all conditions. Here is an exercise to help you train your inner focus.

1. Develop a race plan for each competition and stick to it. Your race plan is your blueprint. Michele's and my race plan was crucial to our victory against overwhelming odds. Some athletes either don't have a race plan or throw it out the window because of flagging confidence or what a competitor is doing. It's okay to modify your plan according to conditions and in consultation with your coach, but don't second-guess it. Stick to the plan you've trained for.

2. After each race, evaluate your focus. Just like you log physical performance results, keep track of your inner focus. Identify where and when you were able to maintain concentration. What were you doing when your focus was solid? Also log where and when you became distracted, whether by pain, external factors or thoughts in your head. What was happening at that point to affect your focus? This has similarities to "An Exercise to Clear the Kink" in Chapter 2. That exercise was related specifically to beliefs whereas this one improves focus.

3. Learn and apply the lessons to the next race. Now, look at your distractions. What can you learn about them? How could you have prepared differently to avoid them? When you get into a similar racing situation, what could you do differently to maintain your focus? Where do you need to strengthen your focus in general, and what steps can you take for the next time you race? Prevention takes a lot less effort than intervention.

Strengthening your focus requires discipline and effort, but it is absolutely worth it.

Chapter 5

Stay Connected to Your Goal

M ost athletes would agree it's important to know what your performance goal is. After all, without a definite milestone you would never know when you had arrived.

Being able to state your performance goal and staying connected to it, however, are two different matters. When faced with a setback or breakdown, many athletes will disconnect from their vision and their goal because they don't recognize the process. They don't realize if they work through the adversity, their breakthrough is right around the corner.

In fact, keeping your vision and goal really clear *enables* you to push through adversity and helps you keep your focus razor sharp. But too many athletes get so bogged down by what's going on for them or they're beating themselves up so much that their goal seems far away.

For instance, Tiger Woods's stated goal is to have 19 Master wins, which would break the world record. As of this writing, he's at 14.

Because of the challenges in his personal life, however, he doesn't appear to be connected to his goal. In the past he played through pain and seemed to know what he was capable of. At this point in time, it appears that his confidence is not as strong, he doesn't get into the zone on command and he doesn't walk into a champion golf tournament knowing he's going to be the first-place winner.

He does still talk about his goal, but there's so much gunk coming up for him right now that he doesn't appear to be able to access it like he used to. Some of his drive has been diluted by the distractions going on in his life as he seems to be recreating his self- and public-image.

If Tiger stays committed to his goal and vision, he can get through this difficult period. He can have his breakthrough. Whether he does remains to be seen.

Another golfer, Isabelle Beisiegel, is a perfect example of someone who's pushed through distractions and dealt brilliantly with adversity. As a rookie in 2005, while touring with the LPGA, she was diagnosed with Grave's disease, had her thyroid removed and went to rehab. This resulted in lost playing time and eventually losing her playing privileges, when her request for a medical exemption was denied.

Rather than rage against any perceived injustice, Beisiegel remained connected to her vision and her goal and kept working toward it. Six years later, in 2011, she earned her non-exempt card, and with it became the first woman to qualify for the men's golf tour in Canada.

She wasn't bigger, stronger or tougher than the other female golfers in the Canadian Qualifying School. What separated her from the rest was her champion mindset. She kept a laser focus on her current shot, tuning out all negativity and trusting her abilities to take her the distance. And so they have.

The Power of Congruency
If you want to stay connected to your goals and have the success you say you want, you also must have congruency, alignment between your goals and your values, between what you present externally and how you feel on the inside. This may be part of Tiger's problem.

If you have any doubt about whether you're being congruent, look at your results. Are you taking all the steps you can to reach your goal or do you freeze, remaining stuck? When there is incongruency between what you say you want and what you do, your actions give the clear picture of what's going on.

For example, a local tennis pro is working with a 17-year-old who has the talent and ability to turn pro if she continues to play. However, her drive is not as strong as her physical capabilities. She doesn't appear to have the desire to push herself to be the best she could possibly be.

At this point, her mother calls a lot of the shots, and it's not clear if she's playing because she really loves tennis and being on the court, or if she's doing it because her mother wants her to be a great tennis player. We won't know for sure until her mother is out of the picture. Like many young athletes, she may connect with her Big Why and find the passion inside herself to compete. If she doesn't find it for herself, she will likely quit competing after high school or college.

Your internal beliefs and values drive you to take action or remain inactive. Worse yet, having a disconnect between your values and goals contributes to sabotage.

Incongruency can also show up when athletes return to play after an injury, but hold themselves back because they fear getting injured again. There's a conflict between their goals and a value about safety and health.

Recently, I was working with an equestrian who does dressage, who had experienced a bad fall during a competition. Her horse stopped before the jump, and she kept on going. Her injury and recuperation kept her out of the ring for quite a while. When she was finally able to return, she recognized a hesitancy on her part as she approached a jump.

She was holding herself back, and her horse was able to sense that and, as a result, wasn't jumping as well as he could have.

To help her realign her motivation with her abilities, we worked on her memory about the injury: her self-blame about putting herself in that situation to begin with, and the guilt she felt about holding herself back from what she knew she was capable of doing. Before long, she was able to realign her values with her goals, and begin again to move up in state rankings.

How Do You Hold Yourself Back?

In fact, many of us hold ourselves back for reasons other than injury. We all have anxieties and things we fear and, as a result, avoid taking the necessary action steps toward the things we say we want. We may not even be aware we're doing it.

Some athletes secretly fear the added responsibilities or increased expectations of others that would come if they moved up in rankings, so they don't take advantage of opportunities that could get them there. Others are afraid of letting people down. Still others don't feel they deserve success, so when opportunities arise, they might not take them.

If you're on a team sport, you may not feel confident that you can pull off a particular play, even though you can, so you let the opportunity go by. I've also seen athletes throw in the towel before they even begin when they think the competition appears bigger, stronger or better prepared. They figure, *Why should I give it everything I've got? I have no chance of winning anyway.*

I've seen athletes, particularly girls and women, not want to beat someone because they don't want that person to feel bad or don't want to leave someone they care about behind or don't want to create conflict in a rivalry situation, so they don't do as well as they could. In those instances there's incongruence between their performance goal and underlying beliefs about how women should behave and values related to being a "good girl" or "nice."

Sometimes athletes don't want to rise up and be more successful because of what they would have to give up. They might have to relinquish some privacy or time with their family. So their values of privacy and family are colliding with their performance goal.

We have all had opportunities we haven't taken because we don't feel we've trained enough or prepared enough or have enough medals hanging on our walls, trophies on the mantel or credentials after our name.

The trick is to bring awareness to what you're doing and not doing and why. We already explored ways to bring underlying beliefs to the surface. It's equally important to do the same with values.

If you have a value that contradicts your goal, you will not move steadily toward your dream. Also, successful goals have to be based upon your values.

Are Your Values and Goals Congruent?

Simply put, values are things you care about. They tend to be the things we keep near and dear to our hearts. Many values will last a lifetime. Others will change according to life circumstances.

Your sport is a value for you. Competing is likely a value.

Since your values drive your actions or inaction, it's imperative that your values and goals be congruent. When they are, your actions support your goals. For instance, I value rowing and I have the goal of being the best I can be in my sport. I support that value by the action of training, including changing my work schedule so I could train six days a week before going to work. My value is congruent with my goal.

Because my hammer thrower client values competing, and his goal is to compete in the Olympics, he's moved twice, once across the country in order to work with a specific coach. Those are actions he took to support his value, which is congruent with his goal.

An athlete with a value of good health for the body would support it through the actions of good nutrition and self-care. These actions would also support his or her goal.

When your values conflict with your goal, your actions will support your values but *not* your goal. Your subconscious is in a tug-of-war with your conscious. Being pulled in two different directions creates a struggle, and success is unlikely.

Sometimes we're not clear on what we really value or we have outdated values we may not be aware of that are affecting our results.

The good news is values are fluid. Some will change as you change, but you can also take a proactive role. You can reframe your core values with something more appropriate for your present circumstances and goals. For instance, I did change my work schedule, but it took me a year to do so because I just couldn't see myself getting up at 5 in the morning. I valued flexibility in my schedule, the ability to stay up late at night and sleep later in the morning. In fact, I was having the experience of values colliding: the old one of flexibility and the newer ones of rowing and fitness training. Eventually, the desire to row with the Women's Racing Team won out. I was fully committed to doing whatever was necessary to be the best I could possibly be. Those new values became so strong that I became willing to reframe the old one.

••Exercise: Are You Congruent?••

As I've said, congruency is key. It's vital to determine what you actually value, so you can decide consciously whether it is working for you. This exercise will help you clarify your values and flush out any incongruencies that are getting in your way.

1. First identify your core values. What do you care about? Again, these could be your sport, family, health, etc.

_____

_____

_____

If you're having a hard time determining if something is a value, ask yourself these questions:

Is it something I care about?

Do I tell others that it is important to me?

Do I support it with my actions?

If not, it's probably not a core value. We support the things we really care about with our actions.

2. Next, what is/are your goal(s)?

_____

_____

_____

3. Do you see any obvious incongruencies between your values and your goals? If not, go on to the next question. If so, skip to number 5.

4. You want your actions to be complementary to your goals. The things you do on a daily basis, are they supportive of your goal and the things you say you care about? If not, you probably have a conflict between a value and your goal. Go back and study or add to your list of values until you see any incongruencies. When you find it go on to questions 5.

If you have no incongruencies, congratulations! Your path to your goal should be clear.

5. It's time to re-examine your values and/or your goals. So often, people have created values and goals for themselves based upon what they think they "should" be doing or what someone else thinks is best for them. This approach might work for awhile, but not for the long run. Spend some time to get really clear about what you care

about and what you truly want to achieve. This is your life.
Live it as you want to live it.

If you find that you have conflicting or outdated values, are
you willing to update them? For example, when Olympic pentathalon gold medalist
Marilyn King was in high school, she trained with a specific
group of athletes. Whenever the coach would leave the field
for a few minutes, the girls she ran with would slow down and
walk the track. Once he returned they would pick up the pace
again.

At that time, track was a social experience for Marilyn.
However, after going to an event and placing 3rd, her goals
began to change. She wondered if she could make it to the State
Championship. With that seed planted in her mind, she began
to think about the state finals more and more. She realized her
training needed to change if she was going to have a shot at it.

Her social value to walk with her friends when the coach
wasn't watching became incongruent with her new goal of being
a state champion. Now she had a conflict. She had to choose
between friendship and competition. She chose competition.

The next time the coach walked off the field, she joined the
girls who continued to run even when the coach wasn't watching.

Whether conscious or not, your values are the foundation
for all your actions. Instead of going through life blindly,
doing things just because that is how it is always done, take
an active approach, choosing the actions that are best for you.
Generalizations don't work. Cookie cutter training doesn't
work either. The more proactive and involved you are, the
better your results.

Further, when your values and beliefs align with your goals,
your actions are in support of your goals and seemingly magical
opportunities present themselves.

Only it's not magic, it's the power of congruency. And it's a
power that's available for anyone who's willing to seek it.

Chapter 6

See Yourself as a Winner with EFT and Visualization

"The significant problems we have cannot be solved at the same level of thinking with which we created them."
—ALBERT EINSTEIN

Seeing yourself as a winner is crucial because it creates the foundation to start making adjustments, even on a subconscious level, to your performance and other actions you take during practice and competitions.

It affects your approach. You begin to step up your commitment and this impacts your perception. Suddenly the things you never considered doing become viable options.

For example, when many athletes compete, their main focus is "not to lose," thus they're likely to stay within their comfort zone and not take many risks.

On the other hand, when you're focused on "playing to win," you will stretch beyond your comfort zone, going for opportunities you might have allowed to pass by if you were just intent upon not losing.

Also, the focus of "not to lose" is about avoidance while playing to win is about flow, moving toward something, which is always easier than avoidance.

Athletes who are focused on not losing tend to be self-critical, whereas athletes who are playing to win tend to speak to themselves in a more positive way. Athletes trying not to lose tend to have an external locus of control, low self-confidence, and they need praise from other people to validate their worthiness. Athletes who play to win have a greater internal locus of control. They focus on actions that are within their ability to control, primarily attitude and execution. They will self-coach.

The ability to self-coach is especially helpful when an athlete doesn't have a direct connection to their coach and a motivational, positive focus is desired.

Look Outside Your Comfort Zone

Most of us do try to solve problems with the same thinking that caused the problems to begin with. People like staying within their comfort zone. Coaches, too, often try to solve problems in their athletes' performance with the strategies they've always used.

The truly committed athlete is going to do whatever it takes to get results, and if there's something a little bit out of the box, that's easy to apply and is effective and gets results, then not being open to doing it is a disservice to yourself.

Yes, I'm talking about EFT, and I'm challenging you to keep an open mind.

Why You May Need EFT

A lot of times, we say things, do things, and set goals that directly contradict what we claim we really want. Often, we don't even know those contradictions exist because they're below the surface. I talked about this before regarding underlying beliefs and values.

You might be highly committed to your goal and passionately want it, so if there is some subtle energy block around it, whether it's a thought, a belief or how you view reality, it's going to put you into a struggle. You probably know athletes who do great during practice, but when it comes to game day, their performance isn't up to par.

It's not necessary to be in that struggle anymore. The old way of thinking had you white knuckling it, toughing it out, thinking your way through it.

But what if toughing it out isn't the solution? What if the problem is deeper, but also easier to shift because it has to do with energy? Think about how you feel energetically on a day when you're practicing and not doing well versus a day when everything is coming together. You feel focused and present. You feel wonderful and it's easy. There's no resistance. Your energy is flowing. Being in the zone is a timeless quality. It's almost as if you can slow down, or speed up, time.

EFT or "tapping" can help you make that shift. It can help you clear any resistance between what you say you want for yourself, where you are now and where you want to be.

It's also an incredibly simple technique you can learn and start using on yourself right away.

How EFT Works

Traditional coaching focuses on actions, thoughts and feelings. EFT, which stands for Emotional Freedom Techniques, works with acupressure points in the body to help neutralize negative emotions around a specific event and correct the flow of energy.

Think of a flashlight with batteries. The batteries have a full charge, but if you put them in backwards, because they're not making the right connection, no matter what you do, the flashlight won't work. However, when you turn the batteries around, there's a clean connection, and the flashlight is going to work beautifully because the energy is flowing.

EFT works in much the same way. You tap with your fingertips on various acupressure points on your body as you focus on a particular emotional or physical issue, and balance is restored, often within minutes.

If you're feeling skeptical, join the club. As I told you before, I was a skeptic, too, until it cured my life-long chocolate addiction.

EFT has been proven successful in thousands of clinical cases and is being adopted by many health care practitioners. It often works where nothing else will.

How Can EFT Help Me?

You may be wondering how EFT can help you improve as an athlete. Remember my client who was teased by the neighborhood kids? Working with him, using EFT, he was able to distance himself from the memory.

EFT didn't erase the memory or change the history of what actually happened. It disconnected the emotions attached to the event. Then, using visualization, we had him turn the games into a positive event. As a result, the old memory, the actual one, lost its power over him.

The incident no longer has any emotional charge for him. He doesn't get triggered anymore. (A trigger is something that happens in the present that reminds you of a past pain and you then react to the present incident as though it were the past pain. You think you're reacting to what's happening in the present, but you're not.) As a result of using EFT, my client is less reactive and more empowered. He has a choice as to how he wants to act or react to any given situation that might formerly have been a trigger.

Also, as a result of the original experience of being taunted by the neighborhood kids, my client formed various subconscious beliefs about having to defend himself and viewing himself as the underdog. Through EFT, we were able to reframe the experience so that he doesn't respond from a child-like perspective to situations where he feels like the underdog. He also created new beliefs about himself, who he is and what he can do.

Another client, a golfer, didn't qualify during a qualifying tournament that would have given him a place on the team during the actual tournament. He beat himself up about it and was very disappointed and self-critical.

We did EFT around being in this challenging situation of having to compete against other teammates to play in the tournament, about his feeling of letting other people down, and being a perfectionist and overly concerned about what people think of him. We were able to reduce the emotional intensity around all of those states. The next time he was asked to qualify for a tournament, he felt more confident and didn't experience the same anxieties. He remembers the disappointing incident, but it doesn't haunt him anymore.

EFT has also been used to cure the yips, which is very much anxiety- and thought-related. Golfers and baseball players, athletes in sports that involve an arm swing, can get the yips, where, instead of a smooth swing, there's a jerk in the motion as the muscles jump. Because athletes have this tension in a particular situation, it comes up over and over. EFT detaches the athletes from their past association with the yips, and deals with the root of the anxiety. The next time the athletes are in a similar situation, they don't have the same response. Their swing is smooth.

What If?

So many people, whether they're athletes or not, live with the burden of *what if*. What if I took more risks? What if I pushed myself a little harder? What if I had had more confidence and taken that shot?

In the 2011 playoffs with the Miami Heat, what if Lebron James had had a strong 4th quarter? What if he knew how to work through resistance and be game-focused? There might have been a very different outcome.

What if you don't try EFT and you can't get out of the struggle? What then?

Even though EFT appears to be unconventional and, even, weird, try it anyway. Be skeptical and try it anyway. If it doesn't work, you have nothing to lose. But if it does work, you've found something very powerful.

In the Appendices are step-by-step instructions as well as samples you can model. If you find you want more help, see my special offer on page 127 for a trial month's membership to The Winners Circle Club.

Take Your Visualizations to the Next Level

Many sports psychologists talk about visualization, a powerful tool for removing barriers and performing at your peak potential. Coaches use visualization with their athletes. Athletes use it on their own, and they're probably getting results from it, however, most people are not experiencing its full potential.

If you learn to visualize the way I teach it in this book it's like having a simulation screen in your head, which you can then access no matter where you are.

If you're not familiar with visualization, it simply means imagining yourself achieving the best possible outcome. You could call it a "mental dress rehearsal." Elite athletes visualize new moves and win competitions repeatedly in their mind's eye. It's a powerful training technique with a very real physical impact.

Visualization works in part because our mind is unable to discriminate between imagination and reality. That's why a dream can seem so real. Visualization creates new neuropathways in your brain in the same way the activity would if you were actually doing it. Repeatedly visualizing your success strengthens those pathways and contributes to actually attaining your goal. In addition, your subconscious mind will begin looking for opportunities to reinforce your visualized reality. You will begin to alter how you hold yourself, the way you respond to other people and how you engage in your sport. The change may be subtle, but over time the shift in your behavior and identity will be substantial.

Olympic gold-medalist Lindsey Vonn uses visualization prior to a competition. She gets quiet and, in her mind's eye, sees herself skiing down the course. I'm not privy to the details of her training, but it would be smart for her to use visualization while working on a new technique as well. She would visualize herself using the new technique in order to speed her transition to it.

Gymnasts rely upon visualization because a lot of moves in their performances are done blind. Visualization, in effect, becomes their eyes. By practicing the move thousands of times in their mind's eye, it becomes very familiar when they are actually doing their routine.

I was working with a group of gymnasts two days before their state championship, and one of the girls was having trouble with a particular move in her floor routine, so I had her visualize doing that part of her routine as she wanted to perform it during competition. She was able to see herself performing it successfully. During the competition two days later, she placed first in the floor exercise.

Another girl on the team was struggling with her back flip on the beam. She didn't have the trust and confidence that she could do it, and kept freezing.

When I asked her to visualize doing the back flip, she couldn't stay focused and see herself doing it. Sometimes if you're struggling with something, you can't visualize yourself doing it either.

Since she couldn't get past the freeze, even in her mind, I had her visualize doing her back flip and freezing, and then we figured out what was going on right at the freeze. Once we worked that out, I had her visualize doing the back flip and landing it perfectly. She was able, then, to see herself doing it.

Later I talked to her head coach, who told me she nailed the back flip during the state competition.

Triathletes also use visualization to shorten the transition time between legs of the race and to develop a game plan for making those quick transitions. They see themselves getting out of the water after the swim, getting to where their bicycle is, and quickly stripping out of their gear and getting onto their bike. Then later when they actually do it, their transition times are faster.

Visualization Can Also Help You With...

In addition to helping you train when using new techniques, work through performance issues, develop game plans, and perform at your best, visualization can also help you in the following ways.

Cope with the unexpected. The more athletes compete, the more likely there will be some type of equipment malfunction or other distraction they can't control. So I encourage my clients not only to visualize themselves performing well, but also to visualize unexpected occurrences and how they could respond to them.

Then when something happens that could rattle them, they're more likely to stay in control and regain their focus quicker than if they hadn't trained for it. This works even if what happens is not what the athlete exactly imagined.

Feel confident at new levels and on new courses. As I've said, as you move up in rankings, the difference between the worst and the best competitor narrows. You might be confident about always being a winner at your current level, but if you move up to a new level, the competition will become tougher, and your confidence might suffer. There might be new or unanticipated challenges. Instead of being caught off-guard, be proactive. Train for your new level by watching the videos of the people you're competing against—or could be competing against—and visualize yourself playing against them and winning.

This is especially helpful when you're transitioning, say from high school to Division 1 college sports or from college level to professional playing.

Visualization is also helpful if you're playing on a new course or a course you find challenging. Just practice seeing yourself playing on it. Then when you actually are, you'll have done it a hundred times already in your mind and you'll show up more confidently. It won't be new.

If you're injured. If you're injured, your goal is to get back into the game. If you visualize yourself playing, training, and competing, you can stay on top of your game and not spend as much time catching up. As you see yourself going through the motions of training, your muscles will twitch in response to the visualization. You'll continue to work those particular muscles and train your body.

Plus, it will give you something to do and focus on, since you feel so useless and frustrated when you're injured and can't play.

I feel compelled to add that EFT has also been used to speed up the healing process for injured athletes. Tapping can help remove any self-blame for becoming injured. It especially works well when combined with visualization. In your mind's eye visualize your body healing the injury while using EFT on the tapping points.

Use Visualization to Achieve Your Goal

Perhaps the most powerful way to use visualization is for achieving your goal. I use visualization to help me become really clear on my goals and create a positive intention.

You harness the power of visualization by identifying your goal, which must be stated in clear, positive terms. Then as if you were really winning your state championship or on the Olympic podium, you see yourself there.

If you find visualization challenging, just do your best. With practice, it will get easier.

The intention of visualization is to make your goal and vision feel real and, over time, make it real. If you're truly serious about moving up the ranks, bring visualization into your training program. Done consistently over time, you will notice the difference. To get you started, try the exercise below.

••Visualization Exercise••

In this exercise, you're going to be working with a goal or vision. Choose one that feels a bit out of reach, but you still believe could be achieved. For example, if you choose a performance goal of running a four-minute mile by the end of next year and you currently run a seven-minute mile, that might be too far of a stretch. You have to believe your goal is possible or your visualization won't work. Instead of visualizing, you'd be engaging in disbelief.

On the other hand, you might be able to see yourself running a 6:30-mile within a year. Don't worry about how you're going to get there. Those opportunities will come later.

1. What is your goal or goals?

_____

_____

_____

_____

2. Describe your goal in a lot of detail. Be specific. Saying you want to be a great runner is not specific enough. There's no emotion attached to it. Instead say, "I want to be ranked top 10 in the state (or in the world)." Or, "I want to compete in all of my events at the Olympics and stand on the podium." Or "I want to play in the major leagues."

_____

_____

_____

—————————————————————————

—————————————————————————

—————————————————————————

—————————————————————————

—————————————————————————

—————————————————————————

3. If you were to actually reach your goal, what qualities, characteristics, and skill sets would you have? To answer this question effectively, it's helpful to study athletes who have reached your goal. Until then, imagine their traits. List all the qualities you would have, in all areas of your life. What compromises would you have made? For instance, if you're training every morning at 5 o'clock, you can't be partying till midnight. Be as detailed and descriptive as you can in order to make it feel real to you.

—————————————————————————

—————————————————————————

—————————————————————————

—————————————————————————

—————————————————————————

—————————————————————————

4. Where will you be when you meet your goal? Try to stimulate all of the senses in your mind's eye. For instance, if you're on the Olympic podium, what does this milestone look and feel like? What details do you notice? How does it smell? What do you hear? What textures can you feel? The more specific you can get, the better the visualization.

_____

_____

_____

_____

_____

_____

_____

5. By what date do you want to reach your goal? Pick a date that is a little sooner than you would like it to be. People tend to perform better when there's a little extra stress or tension. So if you move up the date to where it's a stretch, you're going to have a more focused effort, and you'll get there sooner.

_____

6. Once you have reached your goal, how will you feel about yourself and your ability? What will be different? How will your training change? How will you feel going into a competition?

_____

_____

_____

_____

How to Use Your Visualization

Think of the details above as individual scenes, and then string them together to form a movie for your mind's eye of achieving your goal with ease and confidence. This is your visualization.

Now, play it over and over again. I usually have two to three goals at a time, and I visualize each of them twice a day—in the morning before I get out of bed and in the evening as I'm going to sleep. A visualization on a very specific thing can take a couple of seconds. The visualization above will probably take you about 15 to 20 minutes.

If that sounds like a big commitment, think about your physical training program. How often do you train? How many hours, weeks, months, years are put into training for a particular event? The more you train and the more you repeat it, the more muscle memory you create so that you're responding from a natural, knowing place with ease and confidence when you compete.

The same is true for visualization. As you do it, you come to believe in it more and more, and you move closer to your goal. Also, viewing yourself as a winner becomes more natural to you.

A One-Two Punch: Combining Visualization with EFT

Often people don't really believe they can achieve their goals. As they visualize there's still some doubt in the back of their mind. If you follow your visualization with EFT, you can neutralize the doubt on the spot.

When I work with a client, I frequently combine the two techniques.

I did so with my golfer client who over swung on a par-4 hole

and her ball ended up in a hazard. I mentioned her before—
instead of taking 4 strokes to sink her ball, it took 14. Now, this
is someone who has very high expectations of her playing and,
as the newest person on the team, wanted to do her best and not
let down the team. When she got into the tournament, however,
she wasn't able to shake off the incident, and her confidence was
shaken.

With EFT, we worked on her frustration, anger and disappointment associated with the original incident and also about
having let herself and the team down. Using EFT we first
"tapped" on the self-critical thoughts for getting into this situation in the first place. Saying those statements aloud while
tapping lessens their intensity. After awhile they just don't feel
true anymore.

After the negative thoughts, we focused on her strengths,
continuing to use the tapping to cement in her positive qualities. Then using visualization, with EFT, we restructured her
memory. I had her go through the shot as she wished she had
played it. This lessened the intensity of emotion because now, in
her mind's eye, she got to play it the way she meant to execute
the shot.

EFT and visualization work immediately. One night, just to
introduce myself, I called the hammer thrower who ended up
becoming my client. He told me about the slump he'd been in
all year and mentioned that the next morning was going to be
his last competition of the season. I asked him if he would like
to do some work around that, and he said, "Yes."

He didn't know me. He'd never used EFT before, but he
was willing to try it. That's lesson one of this story—be open to
opportunities when they arise. You never know. Someone could
just call you out of the blue.

We talked for 10 minutes about his core issue, and then
did some tapping around it. While he tapped, I asked him to
visualize how he wanted to throw. Then I helped him with his

mindset and made suggestions of what to focus on as he went into the competition. Being able to get into the zone, at will, changed his mindset.

A couple of days later, I got an e-mail from him telling me that not only did he win his event, but he had a season's best, throwing 12 feet farther than he had all season long!

I have to agree that's impressive, but the much more powerful part of the story is what if I hadn't followed my intuition to call him? That would have been on me. And what if he hadn't been willing to try something new? Given what his season had been like, he probably wouldn't have had the same results the next day, and he would have ended the season on a low note and gone into training for the next season with less confidence. When he started the next season, he might not have believed he could reach his goals. In fact, he told me he was on the verge of walking away from the hammer throw.

Now, he's on the verge of the Olympics. I'm not saying that EFT and visualization can get you to the Olympics, but they can give you emotional distance from what troubles and distracts you—and get you several steps closer to your goal.

To find out for yourself, try the exercise in Appendix V, which will walk you through combining visualization and EFT.

Seeing yourself as a winner is not about how others see you, it is about how you see yourself. If your heart is in the game, if you are committed to excellence and ready to go the distance, nothing can get in your way unless you allow it to.

Seeing yourself as a winner is truly about living your dream. I believe this is why people revere athletes. Athletes pursue their dream, turning it into a reality, whereas most people left their dreams behind long before. Athletes offer hope that anything is possible.

Part Three

Act Like a Winner

Chapter 7

How to Act Like a Winner

Sometimes you have to grow into a position. Acting like a winner helps you grow into *being* a winner.

What does it meant to act like a winner? How do winners act?

The obvious difference is winners go into competitions with the intention to win as opposed to having the focus of "not losing." They have a different perception, frame of reference, and mentality. Winners don't necessarily see failure as others do; they know they can grow from every experience.

They're passionate, always open to learning, and perhaps the most surprising—they know that they don't know it all.

If you've made it this far into the book, then you have at least one vital winning quality—the willingness to learn.

As for the rest, it's not as though you either have it or you don't. You can learn the other traits. In fact, at some colleges, golfers take a personality-type test to see if they have the characteristics of a professional golfer, and if they don't have them yet, they work on developing those things.

In other words, you can learn how to be a winner. And acting like a winner is a great way to start.

How to Act Like a Winner

1. Start Now

A lot of people say, "When this happens *then* I'll make some changes." They put off into the future what they could be doing now. Does that future ever come? Often, no.

It's really important to ask yourself what you could be doing *now* to step into being a winner. This chapter will give you some ideas to help get you started.

Recently, I asked a minor league baseball player why so few players in the farm leagues and in the minors make it to the majors. He said making the move has to do with luck. I disagree.

Luck has nothing to do with it. It has to do with how someone shows up, how and, even, *if* they recognize opportunities, and creating the opportunities to make the "luck" happen.

Let's say a team has three pitchers, and one person is getting played more than the other two. What differentiates him from the pitchers on the bench? What qualities do starting pitchers have? It's not about their character necessarily, but how professional they are, what they've done to improve their stats and how they help the team.

If you want to be a starter, ask yourself if there are things your coach is looking for or the major league scouts are looking for, that you could strengthen in your own play.

2. Study Elite Athletes

How do you figure out what coaches and scouts are looking for? You could ask, but more importantly, you should observe and study the starters as well as those athletes who have already achieved the goal you've set for yourself.

What do these athletes do? What do they offer their coach? How do they train? And how is their lifestyle congruent with consistently playing at a high caliber?

These top athletes live differently on and off the field than you do. They train differently. They might have different ways of taking care of themselves—how they prepare for their competitions, their eating and sleeping regimens. There will be nuances, and you won't know what those things are unless you study the athletes.

Once you find those nuances, see what small adjustments you

can begin making now toward the goal of living and training as they do.

Also, bring those details into your visualization. As you see yourself in your mind's eye doing what they do, you will make incremental changes and your performance will start to shift.

Becoming aware of the day-to-day realities of those athletes will also help you in several other ways:

• It will prepare you to deal with any challenges you'll face later. You won't be surprised, for example, by what you have to give up.

• You learn the qualities scouts are looking for, and, as a result, will rise at a faster rate or get noticed.

• It will create confidence, and confidence is a strategy for subtly intimidating your competitors. Let's just be honest about that.

The bottom line is, if you have a vision of where you want to be, then why not do everything within your power to tilt the odds in your favor?

3. Create Your Own Opportunities

One of the keys to tilting the odds in your favor is to create your own opportunities. You can't wait around to be discovered. You have to be proactive.

If you have your eyes set on playing pro sports and you are currently in college and want to be recognized by a scout, what can you do to get noticed? It depends upon how much play time you're getting. If you're on the bench most of the game, then it's important to be your best during pre-game warm-ups. You never know who might be watching. To get even more attention, join a summer club where other blue-chip prospects might be playing. Be a team player. Go for plays, but make your teammates look good as well.

Even if you are not a naturally gifted athlete, it is still possible to rise to the top. Passion trumps physical ability. Having your heart in your sport, knowing how to deal with adversity and having the willingness to consistently improve your performance are qualities of winning athletes. Natural talent will only take you so far.

Also, talent alone is not enough. Talent must be combined with a strong, deep motivation to take you the full distance.

If you feel you deserve a chance, or would like to be in a different position on the team, the best thing to do is talk to your coach. Discover what qualities your coach is looking for in that position. Learn what you need to do to be considered. If someone better is already in that position, observe that athlete. Where do they excel? What do you need to do to exceed that athlete's talent?

Sometimes enthusiasm sells. Sometimes a coach doesn't see a person as having the physical capabilities to even be on the team, but he or she is so passionate about wanting to play that the passion overrides the lack of obvious physical capabilities.

The bottom line is if you start looking to create opportunities, they will appear.

4. Good Nutrition and Self-Care

If you're looking to be at the top of your game, mental clarity is not optional.

Along with clarity come insights, and insights spring from intuition. Alcohol and recreational drugs impair your intuition as well as your emotional awareness.

I really believe that elite athletes should be alcohol-free and abstain from recreational drug use.

I'm not a nutritionist so I'm only going to say that athletes should and should not eat certain foods. Obvious examples to avoid include soda, energy drinks, chips, high doses of caffeine, tobacco products, fried foods, fast food and highly processed foods.

Elite athletes respect their body as their vehicle and treat it well. If you want to be a top athlete, eat like one and keep your mind clear.

5. Use Keywords

Keywords are quick affirmations, easy reminders of how you want to act as a winner. They create focus and are particularly useful with unfamiliar or counterintuitive behaviors.

Keywords work similarly to sensory memories. For example, if you're a runner and you go to the track for a meet you'll smell freshly cut grass. Then when you go someplace else where there's freshly cut grass, the smell will bring back memories of running.

When using keywords correctly you pair a simple word to a particular action to keep yourself focused on the goal. The more you practice using your keyword to bring up a certain feeling, the more effective it will be. The keyword creates a new neural pathway in your brain, which is activated when you repeat it while doing the activity or in the situation. It is a form of muscle memory. By creating an association, the word creates a behavioral response.

For example, skiing is something I strive to get better at. When I'm focused on the technical parts of what I need to do to make a turn, such as when to lift my leg, when to plant the pole, and how to turn my body, I tend to tense up and fall down. Something I really want to avoid.

So I use the keywords *ease* and *confidence* when I ski. As I make my turn to the right, I say, "ease," and as I make my turn to the left, I say, "confidence." I go down the whole mountain, saying: *ease, confidence, ease, confidence.*

As a result, I'm more relaxed. I'm letting my body do what it knows how to do, instead of trying to control it, and I ski much better.

One of my golf pro clients uses keywords to help with rushing. If he feels rushed early on in a competition, he stays rushed the entire game, which affects his score. Also, if he has a bad shot within the first three holes, it throws off his entire game. He never recovers his focus.

To help him with those problems, we came up with a ritual to remind him to breathe, relax and use keywords to refocus him on how he wants to show up. He uses his keywords, *relax* and *present,* before even taking a step onto the golf course. He also uses them during the game if he has a bad shot. The keywords remind him to compose himself, put the last shot behind him, and refocus on one shot at a time.

I'm using keywords, as well as EFT, in my work with a teenaged tennis player who's very talented and moving up in state rankings, but gets easily frustrated because of his high expectations. He gets angry and stops playing, and his focus and performance go downhill. His behavior was affecting his rankings and isolating him from the other juniors.

We came up with the keywords *power* and *focus,* which remind him how he wants to be on the court. Using the words retrains his brain. He remembers not to take it personally when things don't go his way. If he doesn't play well, it's not about him as a person; playing is a set of actions he takes.

As a result of using keywords, he became more relaxed, letting go of missed shots that normally would have frustrated him. As a result of using both keywords and EFT his anger response changed. He now has more fun and the other players on his team enjoy being around him.

If you'd like to start using keywords right away, see the exercise below.

••How to Use Keywords••

1. Keep it simple.

Often, we want to complicate things, but with keywords, simple will get you the best results.

2. Think about how you want to perform.

If you're not certain, do you know what your coach is asking of you? If my coach wants me to work on something, I trust he sees something about what I'm doing that I can't see, therefore, I try to work on what he's focusing on. Tip: sometimes coaches give too much feedback and it becomes sensory overload, which easily leads to overwhelm. I repeat this just below, but choose to work on only one or two things at a time. You might even want to let your coach know what you are working on so that he or she can support you in those areas.

3. Choose one or two words that have meaning to you about how you want to perform.

Choose as few words as possible. We don't have the capacity to track and maintain focus on a lot of different things. Changing one or two things is all you need to do at a time. So really focus on those one or two things you most want to work on.

_____

_____

4. Try out your word (or words), connecting it to something physical, like I did with skiing, and be willing to modify it, if necessary.

As I said, using keywords is very simple. You're now ready to start using them to help you be the player you want to be.

You Can Do It

If you're wondering whether you can successfully apply these tools on your own, let me tell you about the high school swimmer who came to one of my seminars.

He'd been ranked number 1 in the state, but went into a slump. It had gotten to the point where swimming wasn't fun for him anymore, so he took two years off, which at his age is significant. He went back to swimming, but hadn't achieved the times he knew he was capable of and that were needed to move him up to the next level, to compete nationally.

At the seminar, I talked about acting as if (which I'll share in the next chapter), visualization, keywords, and coming up with a game plan.

The following weekend, I got a call from his mother, who told me he won his next events and achieved the times he had wanted for himself.

If he can get those results after just attending a two-hour seminar, you can get results too.

Chapter 8

Act "As If"

One of the most effective ways to achieve your goal is to act "as if" you already have. You really take it in that you already are the winner you want to be, and then you behave and makes choices as though the future you want is occurring right now. Acting "as if" helps you evolve into your next level of rankings or success.

When you act as if you've already achieved your goal, how you look at and respond to situations transforms. You realize you can choose how you want to act or react.

Old beliefs getting in your way will start to come up. If you're really committed, be open to looking at those beliefs to determine whether they're something you want to hold on to or modify.

For example, one of my golfing clients thought he didn't play as well on narrow courses. I told him this belief was just a distraction, because the width of the course doesn't matter, since the ball is only a couple of inches in circumference.

His belief that narrow courses were more difficult to play was getting in his way, and he had to learn to view them differently. He was willing to modify the belief, and he did it through EFT and reframing.

Acting "As If" Can Give You the Edge

I encouraged you earlier to learn to love what you avoid. Acting "as if" is a great way to accomplish that. In fact, I encourage my track and field clients to learn to love running in the rain by acting as if they do. Everyone else will dislike running in the rain. They'll complain. It will affect their performance, but if my clients learn to love running in the rain, they won't resist it like the other athletes do. While the others are complaining, my clients can't wait to get started. They're happy. The weather doesn't bother them. This is definitely noticed by the other racers, some of whom will be intimidated by their nonchalant attitude. Without even trying, my clients' new stance gives them an edge.

During the process, they will also learn to run really well under any condition, which will make them more versatile.

This strategy is effective for any outside sport where weather has an impact, such as football or soccer.

As I said before, making friends with what you don't like is extremely helpful for any challenge you're facing. Rather than looking at the situation as an obstacle affecting your performance, act as if you love it. This will begin to shift your perspective dramatically and enable you to rise to the challenge, overcoming it with ease.

A Tool for Acting "As If"

A powerful tool for acting "as if" is intention setting. An intention is a goal brought to life by connecting strong, powerful emotions to it. This creates focus and fire and an almost magnetic energy that starts to draw opportunities toward you. Results come at a quicker pace than with just goal setting alone.

Unlike goal setting—which tends to be sterile, with a problem and objective activities, a beginning date and an ending date—an intention is a mindset strategy for utilizing positive focus and expectation to achieve your goals.

If you had trouble with the visualization exercise, it might help you to start here with your intention. Once you create your story of how to reach your goal you might find it easier to visualize the end result. Also, if talking is easier than writing, you can record and transcribe your intention (and your visualization), which would give you both a verbal and written version.

I have training, business and personal intentions. Some intentions are just for one day while others are longer term. For the exercise below, choose whichever category and timeframe appeals to you.

••An Exercise to Create Your Intention••

1. Decide what your goal is. You can use the same one you used for the visualization exercise or choose a different goal.

_____

_____

_____

_____

_____

2. What is your challenge in relationship to your goal? What are you facing? Where are you stuck? Write it here.

_____

_____

_____

_____

3. Choose three to five action steps you could take to reach your goal.

_____

_____

_____

_____

_____

4. Like we did in the visualization exercise, create a story for each action step. How do you feel about it? What are the circumstances surrounding the step. What's the environment? Who is there with you? Who isn't? Make each story as rich in detail as you can. The richer the better, and the more you can bring your senses into it, the more your story will actually come alive.

_____

_____

_____

_____

_____

_____

_____

_____

_____

_____

_____

_____

_____

_____

5. Together these stories comprise your intention. They form a highly personal story of achieving your goal, similar to the storyline of a movie.

There are two schools of thought on what to do with your intention. One says to write it and forget it, letting your subconscious do the work. The other says read the intention every day, keeping it front and center in your conscious mind. Use the approach that makes the most sense to you.

Feel free to modify your intention as your situation changes. Your intention should be a living document.

Desire Is More Important than Knowledge

If you're looking to move up in rankings, you want to set your next goal and create your next intention before reaching your current goal. This reinforces the idea: If you can dream it, it's possible. You don't have to know all the different action steps it will take to reach your next goal. Just get started with what you do know and the steps will come up at the appropriate time.

Having a strong, burning desire is much more important than knowing how to get there.

For instance, Brazilian Marta Vieira da Silva is seen as the best female soccer player in the world; some say she's the best of all time. When Marta was growing up in Brazil, she was very poor. There was no place for girls to play soccer and the boys didn't want her either, but that didn't stop her. She played by herself with an old soccer ball until she wore it out. She couldn't afford to buy a new ball, so she made one out of paper, plastic, and string and kept practicing by herself.

Eventually, the boys let her play when they were desperate for another warm body, and then, when they realized how good she was, they let her play with them more often. When a women's team started in Brazil, she played with the team until it disbanded, and eventually was picked up to play in the United States.

When she was playing with the boy's team, she played barefoot because she didn't have enough money for shoes. When she went to the women's team, the Brazilian coach gave her shoes, but they were two sizes too big.

Now *that* is a burning desire to play—building your own ball and playing in shoes two sizes too big.

You may not have such a dramatic story, but I bet you have your own burning desire for your sport. Bring it into your intention. The more emotion attached to your intention, the more powerful it will be.

Uplevel

Another tool for acting "as if" is upleveling. In this context upleveling means to upgrade aspects of your performance to reflect the next level of what you're striving toward. You start to make changes now to affect how you feel about yourself and the way you are perceived.

Those changes may be small, mundane and inexpensive. Or they might require investing in something to position you for success.

One of the most powerful uplevels you can do is to work out or train with athletes who are better than you.

If you're ranked in the top five in the state or nation, and you want to be number one, see if you can train with the number one person for a week. You don't know how athletes at the next level train unless you spend time with them.

The differences between what the first ranked athlete is doing and what you're doing probably won't be drastic, because, as I said, as you move up in rankings the difference between the best and the worst narrows, but there will still be nuances or fine-tuning you could apply to your training. There will be things you didn't even know you weren't doing. Training with someone ranked higher than you is a great way to find out what you don't know.

If it's not possible to train with the person, reach out by email or phone and see if you can have a conversation. Or get together at a meet. Some athletes will be open to helping you, others won't.

If the athlete is not open to it, observe the person when you're at a common meet. Notice what time the person got there. How did he or she warm up differently than you? Did he or she do anything right before the competition to prepare for it mentally? What did the athlete do after the competition?

Look for what the athlete is doing and also what the athlete is *not* doing. Sometimes that's much more telling. Is the person *not* spending a lot of time around teammates? Not warming up like everybody else does? If so, he or she might have modified something in the training program to give him or her an edge.

As I said before, traditional training works for the average athlete. If you want to be extraordinary, you have to train differently. Top athletes often modify the rules to what's best suited for them.

Once you have found your top-ranked athlete and know some things you didn't know before, take the information and see how you can modify it to make it work for you. You might find you don't want to do some of the things the athlete does, but others things will be gems.

Even a small change can make a significant difference in your training and confidence. You might find yourself willing to do things you weren't willing to do before.

For instance, when I was interviewed as an expert in the *Los Angeles Times* to comment on the television show "Necessary Roughness," it empowered me to reach out to people who were better known in the field and to possible business partners I didn't feel comfortable reaching out to before.

You might find your upleveling experience empowers you, as well, to take risks you shied away from in the past.

Change Is Significant

Whether big or small, any changes you make will be significant. Acting "as if" isn't always comfortable. You may be outside of your comfort zone, stretching yourself.

A champion mindset will prepare you for taking those necessary steps for success, no matter how uncomfortable you might feel.

Your change will lead to growth, which can be rapid. Too often athletes are not ready for fast growth and they act out to sabotage it. There is an implosion effect. What do I mean by that? Well, when something happens too quickly and the foundation is not in place, it is likely to fall apart. It becomes messy because some things might not have been foreseen and prepared for, which leads to collapse or major setbacks.

The best way to handle growth is to know you don't have to do it all on your own. Go find the right support. Where to find the support you need is the subject of the next chapter.

Chapter 9

Choose Your Best Team

Who Is On Your Team?

Athletes are not islands unto themselves. They typically don't train alone, figure it all out by themselves or coach themselves to victory. Your "team" is actually a big group. It includes all of the people you associate with: your coach and other trainers, team members, athletes you turn to for help in working through a challenge, other support people, family and friends.

The members of your team have the power to raise you up or bring you down. If you have support people who are always critical of you or negative, it's easy to get discouraged. I've seen athletes throw in the towel because after you've been beaten down enough you may begin to believe it. Other people do have the fight in them to prove the person wrong, but not everyone does.

Sometimes the lack of support is subtle. For instance, family members might be supportive of you generally, but they might not believe in your dream or your big goals as strongly as you do. Or one of your goals might compete with theirs. For instance, if your training schedule requires you to travel and your husband or wife wants you to stay home, there's a conflict.

Or, family members might say things like, "Are you sure you want to do that?" Or, "You might not want to do this because you might not win."

You need to understand where those responses originate. Those family members want you to have your vision, but they're afraid that seeing you frustrated or disappointed when you don't meet your expectations will be uncomfortable for *them* and they won't know how to deal with it.

When you get frustrated or disappointed, they believe they're supposed to do something about it, but it's not their purpose or responsibility. Their purpose in your life is to validate the experience you're having and to support you in doing whatever is necessary and right for you, not what *they* believe is right for you. Nobody is the expert on your life or what you need more than you are.

It is important for you to absorb good advice or insight from other people, but the bottom line is you need to make any decisions for yourself. If you don't take an opportunity, you're the one who may spend the rest of your life wondering *what if.*

Not long ago, I was talking with a former professional basketball player, now a businessman, who was facing opportunities and challenges and having some confidence issues.

I asked him if he had similar issues when he was playing basketball, and he said he did. He wondered how different things would have been if he had taken advantage of certain opportunities or pushed himself a little bit harder or taken more risks.

In his business career, he sees some parallel processes occurring with his confidence, and he wants to do it differently this time.

An athlete's career, for the most part, is pretty short-lived. Eventually, you're going to move on to something else. How you show up while competing will probably be pretty similar to how you move into a new professional career.

If you have confidence issues, if you hold back, if you are afraid of change, those things will likely come up again in your profession until you look at why they're happening and decide to modify the underlying beliefs to those more appropriate for your life right now.

Does Your Team Mirror the Winner in You?

"You are the average of the five people you spend the most time with." —Jim Rohn

Does that quote scare you? If so, you might want to consider this section carefully. The people you surround yourself with will affect your mindset. If you are spending time with people who are forward thinkers and who understand your excitement and drive, you are in good company.

You want to connect with people who are already achieving some of the goals you are currently striving for. If you want to be a millionaire, you need to spend time with millionaires. They think differently and act differently than people living paycheck to paycheck.

The same is true of elite athletes. If you want to perform at a higher level of play than you're currently performing at, start spending time with athletes who are already at that level. Befriend them. Hang out with them. Notice how they spend their time. Notice what they do and don't do.

On the other hand, if you are surrounded by people who are always in one crisis after another and you seem to be the solution to their problems, your energy will be drained. Or if you are very competitive, wanting to stretch yourself, but others on your team play for a different reason—maybe it's social for them—you are likely to not push yourself as hard as if you were playing with people who have the same ambition as you. This is particularly true of high school and recreational teams. This can lead to frustration and resentment on your part and poor teamwork for the team.

One of the most difficult things to do, but also necessary for moving forward is to look at the people in your life. Highly-dedicated athletes sometimes feel conflicted when they have to make difficult decisions about who to spend time with, whether it's friends, family, teammates or coaches. The athletes are moving on and sometimes they have to create distance between themselves and people they are attached to emotionally because, otherwise, the relationships would sabotage their goals.

This is not easy to do. But as my husband, Steve Fogelman, says, "You measure personal growth by the people you leave behind."

You may have to limit contact with people who bring you down or who can't support your vision 100% or who drain your energy.

There may be people in your life you care about, say in your family, whom you're not going to cut out of your life entirely. In that case, it's even more important to set boundaries with them and have a strong support system of positive people around you.

When you're on the journey toward excellence, you must have positive people on your team, people who share in your dream because you will definitely face obstacles and challenges along the way. And although you're persevering, if you're not having the results or seeing the progress you expect, doubt might begin to creep in.

That's when your group of supporters, who really believe in you and your vision, are so important. They will lift you up when you can't hold yourself up.

If you don't have those positive people in your life who can help you refocus on your strengths, you might get frustrated, and then the negative people in your life, who so easily point out flaws and criticize, might reinforce your doubt, digging it in deeper, which will keep you in the place of doubt longer than is necessary.

Yes, I said "necessary." When you're feeling doubt, you might actually be at the threshold of a breakthrough, but you can't see it. Your supportive people, however, are able to partner with you to help you process through what's happening and also what's preventing you from taking the leap of faith in front of you. They might also take the leap of faith with you. Remember, you don't have to do it on your own.

We all need people on our team to help us see what we can't. None of us can see what's right under our nose. We get caught up in our own story and it's hard to see it from another perspective.

How Supportive Relationships Help

There's a classic psychological concept called the Johari window, which explains the power of any supportive relationship, including marriage.

Picture a window with four quadrants.

In the first quadrant are the things you know about yourself and others know about you too. These are easily observable things, such as what you look like.

In the second quadrant are your secrets. You know these things about yourself, but I don't. For instance, you may eat a pint of ice cream every night or watch a soap opera. These are things you may not want anyone else to know.

In the third quadrant are hidden things. You might not know these things about yourself, but I do. Body language, although it might be subconscious, is stronger than the spoken word. For example, if you're anxious about your upcoming tournament you might nervously tap your right foot without realizing it. The hidden thing could also be my opinion about you.

The fourth quadrant contains the unknown. These are the things you don't know about yourself and I don't know either. These are your subconscious thoughts, dreams you don't recall, repressed memories, things that happened when you've dissociated or "spaced out."

As you're working with a coach (or a counselor or other supportive people), unknown, hidden or secret things come out into the open and those quadrants get smaller, while the first one becomes more expansive. Through the process of insight, feedback and processing, you become aware of things about yourself you never would have known or you take what you knew to a deeper level.

The result is a more expansive open window for you. Supportive relationships have the power to help us grow tremendously.

What If You Are Surrounded by Negativity?

Who wouldn't want a cadre of people helping them at every turn? But what do you do if you don't have positive support in your life right now? What if the only one who believes in your dream is you?

If so, don't despair. Remember Michael Jordan? As a sophomore he tried out for varsity but was too short. But he believed in himself and kept playing.

Your own support is a potent beginning. Now you can start looking for your team. If you look, you will find.

In the meantime, here are a few other practices to help you, and even those with great support systems will strengthen their edge.

How to Cope with a Negative Coach. Having a coach who truly knows how to motivate you and believes in you and is able to believe in you even when you can't believe in yourself at the moment is very powerful.

Too often, however, coaches focus on what you're not doing well. They don't always realize you need to be told what you are doing well.

A golfing client felt that his performance was being hampered by his coach during tournaments because the coach was only telling him what not to do, where not to hit the ball. My client believed the negative coaching was defeating the purpose of coaching, and causing his performance to drop.

Another coach I heard about threatens to stop coaching team members if they don't improve, but those athletes weren't being coached on how they could improve their performance. They were just being told what not to do.

Negative coaching is counterproductive. Focusing on the negative enhances the negative. If you want to improve you have to focus on areas to improve. To me this is common sense and it's borne out by the most recent neuroscience.

However, if your coach is negative, there are ways to cope with it. I said some of this before, but it bears repeating.

First and foremost, understand that your coach truly wants you to succeed. Your success is a reflection on him or her.

Second, rather than avoiding the issue and letting frustration build up or blaming your coach, look for solutions. Try to communicate your experience to your coach. He or she may not realize the negative impact on you.

Or, if you need something from your coach you're not getting, like my hammer thrower client, find someone who can help you with that aspect of your training.

Third, if you can't switch coaches, look past the negativity to find the gem in the feedback. I encouraged my golfing client to take the gist of the advice and see how his coach was trying to support him or encourage him even though it was coming out the wrong way. I also told him it was a great opportunity to learn how to not let anybody else's energy or negativity get under his skin and affect his performance.

If you can learn to do the same with the negative people in your life, you are one step closer to the freedom that comes from not being negatively affected by what other people do or say.

And if you look at the negative people in your life as opportunities—or inducements—to build your own support team, you can thrive in any environment.

Set the Tone for Your Day. When you spend time with people who tend to be critical or negative, you might not even realize it because you become so used to it. On the other hand, when you spend time with people who are positive and really doing something for themselves or believe in what you're doing, you have a very different frame of mind and experience.

One of the ways to start to control your environment and not let other's negativity affect you is to set your own tone for the day.

Do you start the day reading or listening to all the doom and gloom in the news? If so, that's the tone you're setting for the rest of the morning and even the day.

When you start your day with how people are struggling and not doing well, your brain reinforces that by looking for struggle and things not going well. However, if you don't read the newspaper or listen to the news in the first part of the day, you're setting yourself up for a very different experience.

You can take this further by choosing to start your day with an intention, visualization, meditation, workout or some other aspect of self-care. If you do, you're consciously setting the tone for your day with action steps toward your goal. And that will have a very different affect on the rest of your day.

You don't have to take my word on this. Do an experiment and see for yourself. If you tend to listen to the news every morning, for the next week notice how you are after listening to the news and how long it affects you. Then the following week, instead of the news, read or listen to something motivational.

See if you notice the difference in how you train, how you respond to people, and how you feel about the state of the union.

Create an Internal Support System. Whether you're surrounded by negative people or not, it's powerful to be able to refer to an internal support system. It's almost like having your own personal board of directors.

What do I mean?

First, I want you to open your mind, because this might sound weird at first. I can tell you, though, it works.

I'm suggesting that you visualize yourself sitting with mentors you would choose to have as your guides, and imagine having conversations with them and then listen to their insights. You'd be surprised by the information you can garner this way.

Think of it as your virtual King Arthur's round table, and all these people are there to help support you, give you insights and guidance toward your goal. Who would be sitting at your inner round table?

The truth is as you work towards excellence in whatever you do, intuition is part of the process. How many times when playing a sport have you just "known" to move in a certain way or that an opening was going to occur to give you an edge? The insight wasn't based upon anything conscious. You just "knew."

You can tap into this knowing anytime you want.

Your inner round table is especially helpful when you're facing doubts. That's when you start saying critical things to yourself, a practice you likely inherited from the people who raised you. Some part of you is pointing out all the reasons why you should back down and why you're not supposed to be doing this, or how you don't deserve it.

Doesn't it make sense to replace the practice you inherited with a committee of your choosing, who will champion for you and help guide you?

Napoleon Hill, author of *Think and Grow Rich,* describes nightly meetings with his inner board of directors, which was comprised of figures from history. Through their conversations, he gained insights and wisdom to help guide him on his own personal journey.

If you would like to give it a try, here's an exercise to get you started.

••An Exercise to Create
Your Own Inner Round Table••

1. Make a list of the people you admire most and whom

you would like as guides. They can be living or deceased, famous or not. You can have as many as you want, but in the beginning aim for around four to keep it simple.

_____

_____

_____

_____

2. Sit down, close your eyes, and imagine your group sitting around the table, and start asking questions. It's probably better not to take notes because you might distract yourself from the visualization. Just write down your insights or "ahas" soon afterward.

Don't get hung up on where the information is coming from or whether it's "real."

If you're gaining insights you wouldn't have had otherwise, what does it matter where it originates?

The bottom line is you're able to access a deeper knowledge within yourself by going through this process than if you never would have gone through it. It's just one more way to step out of the box.

_____

_____

_____

_____

_____

_____

_____

_____

_____

_____

_____

_____

_____

3. If you draw a blank or have other difficulty, keep trying anyway. After a week of "training," you might find yourself suddenly engaging in conversations with your round table while you're in the shower or driving the car.

Don't despair, though, if you don't get any immediate results. Just like all new things, there is a learning curve and it requires patience and practice. Remember, this strategy strengthens your intuition, or gut feeling. If you haven't been exercising that muscle until now, it just takes time. Ask a specific question, relax, see what pops up. Forcing something usually gives the opposite response, preventing it from working. Once you get the hang of it, this will be one of your best self-coaching tools.

If it doesn't work for you after a week or so, you can always scrap it. But if it does work, you'll have one more tool to give you an edge you didn't have before.

Adopt the Mantle of the Winner

This section has been about the merits of acting like a winner and how to do so. I've told you acting like you're already a winner changes your focus. You start looking for opportunities, for how you can push yourself, perhaps by taking action where you normally wouldn't, and it changes how you perceive your surroundings.

Acting like a winner also focuses your energy positively and you show up with more confidence, which your competitors will sense. Therefore, not only does acting like a winner change how you see yourself, but how other athletes see you as well.

Part Four

Be the Winner
You Want to Be

.

Chapter 10

Begin Winning Now

To be the winner you want to be, I urge you to take the points I've given you in this book and start to combine them. Don't do this in a way that overwhelms you. You don't have to do it all at one time or perfectly.

These are the three most important changes to make right away:

1. Your belief system. The changes that need to be made in your belief system may have already come up for you. What are they? Or, you could ask yourself: What situation would I like to look at differently? How would I prefer to view it? And how can I begin to make that change?

2. Believe in your goals. Look at your goals and really begin to believe they are possible. Then, rather than focusing on how much work it might take to get there or wondering whether you ever will, start looking for opportunities to meet them. Your goals might be a stretch for you, but if you are fully committed, you will get there.

3. Incorporate a couple of things from your research. Once you've done your research of how elite athletes in your sport think differently and how they approach self-care—which is different from how they *do* things—find a couple of things that you can begin to incorporate now that would make you feel like a winner.

That could be as simple as splurging on a really good pair of shoes or a piece of equipment that the best athletes are using. Perhaps, normally you wouldn't buy the item because you might feel you haven't earned it yet, but if you go ahead and buy it and use it now, your confidence will rise a notch. You'll start feeling like a winner. You'll start to grow into your bigger vision of yourself.

All of these incremental changes, combined with your physical training program, will build upon themselves. They'll come together and create exponential, positive results.

Please note that you do have to use these concepts along with your physical training program. No matter how powerful your mindset, you can't win a marathon if you haven't physically trained for it because you wouldn't have the endurance. Your physical training has to be in place. Having a champion mindset *in tandem* with the physical training is what gives you the winner's edge.

Outcome vs. Performance Goals

Most athletes have outcome goals for times, speed, or distance. They want to do something by a certain time or have a certain amount of hits or be able to run a specific distance. Outcome goals are helpful for knowing if you're hitting your numbers; however, I would urge you to put most of your attention on execution or performance goals, on *how* you're doing what you're doing. Unlike outcome goals, which may depend in part on the competition, luck of the draw, etc., performance goals involve things you can completely control: your mindset and your execution.

For example, every time you practice or compete, set a goal that has to do with having a positive attitude regardless of what's going on or being able to stay focused for a certain amount of time or about your rhythm and tempo, whatever is appropriate for you.

What performance goal would you choose to focus on first?

Also set goals based on technical ability, focusing on those things you have absolute control over. Is there a particular technique you could improve upon, knowing that it will improve your overall performance? Look at your stroke, form or stance. Maybe it's starts, turns or transitions. Decide what you want to focus on first.

As a result of focusing on your performance goals, you will actually be more likely to reach your outcome goals, because performance goals are empowering.

With an outcome goal, you either hit it or not. You succeed or you fail. But an execution goal is about the process, it's about improving, and that keeps you moving forward.

Also, being overly focused on your outcome goal, your score or your ranking, or how you stand in relation to the competition, can be a distraction during events. If you're thinking, *I have to score ten more points to be in the running,* you're not in the moment. You feel anxiety because you're not competing against yourself anymore. You tense up, and your performance drops.

That's an example of a thought's direct physiological impact on your body, and it can happen in a split second.

If you don't hit your outcome goals, you may not only feel anxiety, but also disappointment.

If, on the other hand, you're focused on an execution goal, you're in the moment with the process and you're not bringing the judging mind or the critic into the equation.

If you're focused on improving, you'll *keep* improving, and you're more likely to hang in long enough to start seeing the results that are reflected in your outcome goals.

Personal Best

Being competitive is a natural part of being an athlete. But when competing to win, you are going to fail somewhere along the way. If your sole focus is on winning, it will motivate you for awhile, but it will not take you the full distance to reach your goals. To really remain motivated for the long run requires shifting your focus from winning against the competition to doing your best.

Don't get me wrong, winning is great, but it is an outcome goal. It's just not within your full control to win each and every time. There is only one winner for each event. Winning is a gigantic boost to self-esteem, but if you judge your capabilities by winning, and you don't win, over and over again, you might lose confidence.

Comparing your performance, and where you place, to your fellow competitors has a purpose. It let's you know where you stand. Winning is important if you are on your way to becoming a champion. It builds confidence, but when it occurs too easily, it can also lead to complacency and lack of focus. It is a two-edged sword.

The shift from winning to personal best sets you up for success. Setting goals to improve your personal best provides immediate feedback after each and every event. You might not go home with first place, but noticing performance gains builds confidence and strengthens drive.

With this mindset even losing can be a strong motivator to succeed. You combine that with the commitment to do whatever is necessary to improve and you become even more effective.

When you keep your focus on your personal best, you're always competing against yourself and never against the other team. Competitions and trainings then become opportunities to push yourself to go beyond where you've gone before.

Ironically, forgetting about the competition and focusing on improving personal performance is the fastest way to actually begin beating the competition.

You do have to keep in mind that stretching yourself means you risk failure or a setback, so you have to be willing to fail, and to view those failures as learning opportunities.

As I've mentioned, whenever a new technique or strategy is

introduced into your routine or performance, there is typically a setback or failure. Your performance may temporarily get a little worse, because your brain is rewiring itself, creating new neuropathways, as it sets the framework for moving forward again.

You're creating the opportunity to excel beyond where you were before, so your body and brain need some time to get ready to implement the new approach, concept, or strategy.

But if you are aware of that process and are patient with yourself, you'll experience the leap in performance that makes it all worthwhile.

How to Change

As you integrate the material in this book, keep your focus on the performance goal of *improving* as opposed to having a specific outcome. I know that's a challenge. We've been conditioned to focus on outcome goals, but unless you pair them with performance milestones along the way they will work against you in the long run.

This work is a process, a practice. It's unlikely that you're going to read this and the next time you go out and play, you're going to have a whole new approach to your game. Let's face it, you've been doing your sport one way for a long time, and it takes time to integrate new material and make new habits.

It's also important to acknowledge that change is easier for some people than others, and we all have our own timelines for it. The key is to be open to change, however long it takes you to actually make it.

Also recognize that how you do *anything* is how you do *everything*. If you're stopping yourself from improving your performance, where else are you stopping yourself? Remember the businessman I spoke to who was facing in his business some of the same issues that had held him back in his basketball career? He came to me because he was fed up and finally willing to change.

The good news is the reverse is true as well. If you change how you do *something* that change will reverberate in all areas of your life.

A Model to Help You Change

To help you decide which changes to make from this book, I suggest you apply the following criteria, which is based upon the Stages of Change Model by Proschaka, DiClemente and Norcross. The researchers studied how people make changes in their life, whether consciously or unconsciously, and found that when people go through the following process, they're more likely to actually make the changes and have longer lasting results.

1. **Pre-contemplation stage.** In this stage, you ask yourself if you even have an issue or a problem. For instance, did you resonate with the material about outcome vs. performance goals? Is your focus on outcome goals a problem for you? If it's not a problem, you're not even going to consider making any changes.

2. **Contemplation stage.** If you've passed the first stage and you think the material could help you, but you're not sure, do some research about it. This is an education phase. This book itself could be part of your contemplation stage about whether changing your mindset and limiting beliefs could be helpful to you.

3. **Preparation stage.** In this stage you develop your game plan. You've decided that the change is a good idea, and now you want to think about how you could use the approach and make it work for you.

4. **Action stage.** This is when you start implementing the new approach. The action stage takes a lot of energy because you're focused on whether or not you're actually using the new approach, and if you realize you're not, you take corrective action to put it into play again. This stage has a learning curve and is largely trial and error.

5. Maintenance stage. You've incorporated the new approach into your training or strategy and it's easy now because you're used to it. You have a new behavior, a new approach, and a new mindset.

Take Personal Responsibility

When you make the choice to bring something into your training or competition, as opposed to a more passive approach where you're being told what the next steps should be, you become more involved in your training and have more of a sense of ownership of it, and that changes how you see yourself.

Your self-confidence rises. When your self-confidence rises, your performance likely improves because you start taking risks that you might not have taken when you were a more passive participant. There's also a shift in the dynamic with your trainer or coach. You become partners with the people supporting you.

I'm urging you to be active in your success. If your aspirations are to be the best you can possibly be, then you must take personal responsibility for your training and performance. Don't blame the conditions, your coaching or your equipment.

If your coach tells you to do something and it's not necessarily the best way for you to get results, you have an obligation to yourself, your goal, and your performance to either figure out how to make the guidance work for you or approach that person with what you think is the better route. If you do the latter, together you might see if what you were told to do can be expanded upon, or adapted, so that you can gain from it after all.

The Opportunities Are Already There

One of the many advantages to being active in your success is you're more likely to recognize opportunities. The truth is, when you're looking to move up in rankings, the way to do it is already available to you, and it's probably been there all along. Until now, you just haven't been ready for it so you haven't seen it, or maybe you didn't see it as an opportunity. You might have seen it as something fearful and avoided it.

For example, I was speaking with a freshman high school volleyball team, and the girls told me that they're intimidated when they compete against taller girls.

I suggested that they become comfortable with what seems uncomfortable, and the way to do that was to see if they could practice with the senior varsity team because that would get them used to performing against taller players. It would take away the emotional charge and also stretch their capabilities. It would also help the varsity girls, because teaching what they know would help to ingrain their own knowledge in a different way than just acting upon it.

When I presented the idea, the girls resisted initially. They were concerned that the varsity team would criticize them for not being great players.

I pointed out that those varsity girls were once freshmen themselves and, if they approached them from the standpoint of wanting to learn from them, the girls would see it as a compliment and be willing to help mentor them.

If they take my advice, the younger girls will learn that they can face their fears, and by facing them, the fears will lose their power.

This is a very simple solution to their problem, but it did require the girls to be honest with me, and they will have to ask for help.

The opportunities around you are probably similar. They likely require you to face a fear or two and be open to looking at a situation in a new way.

Leaving Your Comfort Zone Is Liberating

Whenever we view something as an obstacle, whether it's conscious or not, we put a lot of energy into avoiding it. That's why I urge you to view obstacles as opportunities. It opens you up to the simple solution that's been staring you in the face all along.

It also opens you up to personal growth. If you view your

obstacle as an opportunity you head straight for it, facing what you need to face and growing in the process.

For instance, early in my rowing career, I recognized that I was holding myself back from opportunities because I didn't know if I would perform them well. I was concerned about being judged. That was not helping me to become a better rower.

Working on my internal obstacles was a liberating experience. My performance improved. I felt more confident. I was also seen differently by coaches and teammates because, no matter what I was asked to do—even though a part of me wanted to say no at first—I always showed up and did it.

I learned things about myself—about my fortitude and resilience, determination, and how competitive I am—that I never would have known if I had just avoided those things and stayed in my comfort zone.

How Do You Decide Which Opportunity to Embrace?

Taking this back to personal responsibility for a moment, you don't necessarily say yes to every opportunity that comes along. Some might not be right for you at the time.

When an opportunity is presented to you, ask yourself if it is aligned with helping you progress toward your goals. If it is, and it feels like the time is right to do it, then step up to the challenge. If it's not going to help you reach your goals, you don't have to do it.

If fear is the determining factor of whether you take advantage of an opportunity, you end up with a pretty small life and career.

That's not to say you don't consider the risks. Fear serves a purpose. For instance, I wouldn't skydive. You have to look at the fear. What is it about really?

Once you do that, it usually becomes clear whether it's a fear you want to respect.

Mindful Performance

Reflexively kowtowing to fear is a reaction to that fear. When you're in reaction in general, some outside stimulant has activated beliefs, thoughts and emotions, and you then turn to behaviors you've had for a long time that might not be best suited for the situation at hand.

When you perform mindfully, however, you're in action, not reaction. Rather than relying upon outworn behaviors, you rely upon your attitude and your execution.

You set yourself up for mindful performance by anticipating challenges that might come up and having a game plan for dealing with those situations.

If you think about it, much of the "unexpected" is actually somewhat predictable. It usually involves the competition, equipment malfunctions, delays with the start time, etc. And just for the fun of it, if you want to see those unexpected moments firsthand, go to Youtube.com and search for the worst moments in your sport. It is amazing what you'll see.

You can then use that information to your advantage. Come up with your emergency game plan now for what you would do if any of those worst case scenarios happened to you.

Thoughtful preparation is the key to a quick recovery for the bloopers athletes experience when competing. When you think through what might happen during your competitions and develop a game plan to deal with them, you feel more prepared and confident. And then when something "unexpected" does occur, it doesn't throw you off.

In fact, you feel empowered and relaxed. When you're relaxed, you're better able to use the critical thinking skill of looking at all the options and coming up with the best one.

Even if the situation isn't exactly the same as the ones you anticipated, it's likely to be similar enough that you're able to choose how you want to respond as opposed to falling into an automatic reaction.

For example, in the spring, rowing conditions can change

without warning. I might start out with very clear and calm water conditions, and then all of a sudden the wind kicks up, and I might be 20 minutes away from the dock, having to row back against white caps.

The first time that happened when I was in a single, I was ahead of everybody else, and the only thing I could do was turn around and go back, fighting the waves. I could have panicked as the water came over the gunnel and into the boat, but that wouldn't have helped me at all.

I also knew that strong arming wouldn't help, so I just decided to keep as steady of a pace as possible and remain as calm as I could.

The truth is I could have easily capsized since the boats only sit about 2 to 4 inches above the water, and they're very narrow, but I had my plan and enough skill to know how to align my boat with the water and was able to make slow, steady progress.

My experience and my plan prepared me for this particular situation even though I'd never been in one like it while rowing by myself.

Just the process of thinking things through can help you avoid panic when the unexpected happens because you're in the habit of thinking critically and looking for solutions.

Using the quicksand analogy, you may not know what to do, but if you don't panic, you might be able to see a way out of the quicksand. There might be a branch nearby and if you think critically you might be able to find a way to get that branch. If you're in a panic or are highly anxious you don't have access to your critical thinking skills.

Will You Go for the Brass Ring?

I've covered a lot of ground in this volume, but the bottom line is this: Will you decide to go for the brass ring?

In the olden days, merry-go-rounds had brass rings placed along the edge of the structure, just out of reach. If you grabbed that brass ring you earned a prize.

To grab the ring required a literal stretch as well as a stretch of your comfort zone because, if you missed it, you might fall off the horse. But if you could strategize and time it correctly, and try a few times, you might be able to figure out exactly the right timing and angle of reach to be able to stay on your horse, but reach out far enough and grab the ring.

Before you grab the ring, however, you have to make the decision to try. You have to ask yourself: Is this an opportunity for me or not? Once you decide to reach for the brass ring, your brain will start to look for the opportunities to help you stretch yourself and grab hold of it. But it all begins with a decision.

Are you going to grab the brass ring? Are you going to be more open to opportunities? Are you going to turn the page and take the first step?

Are there things that you could be doing to improve your game that you're not doing yet? Is it worth it to have a temporary setback in order to take a great leap forward in the long run?

People who are afraid of disappointing themselves or others or of making mistakes are not as likely to push themselves or step forward in that way, because their inner critic is telling them all the reasons why they shouldn't be doing it.

Winners push forward anyway. They see the opportunity to improve their performance as just the next step to reaching their goals. They get excited by the challenge.

How do you view challenges? Do they bring up fear or apprehension? Do they bring apprehension and then action? Or do they just motivate you to take action?

Obviously, the third response is preferable, but as I've shown throughout this book, change is possible. Change begins with a decision. You can choose to change your approach and take action on things that you wouldn't have taken action on up until now.

You Are a Winner

If you really want something and you know in your heart that's what you ought to be doing, then stay true and committed to it no matter what anybody else is saying.

Your conviction and your connection to your Big Why, your motivator, will take you the distance.

Whether or not you actually reach your loftiest goal, you will meet others along the way. The fact that you took action and a no-excuses approach makes you a winner. And you'll end up being a better person all around because of that choice.

Chapter 11

Your First Step

Many people go to seminars or read books that provide a lot of information, but then they get overwhelmed, because the book or seminar didn't tell them how to get started, and so they don't start anywhere.

I want to make sure that doesn't happen to you, so here is your first step:

Get a piece of paper and write "GOAL" at the top. We're going to use it as an acronym. Then down the left side of the page, take it letter by letter and answer the following questions.

G represents your goal. What is the achievement that you want to have by a particular point in time?

O represents all the obstacles in the way of that goal. What are the "yes, buts," the excuses or the reasons why you shouldn't be trying to achieve your goal? You may say these things to yourself, or other people may say them to you.

A represents all the possible action steps that you could take to reach your goal. Let yourself imagine what they might be. Don't censor yourself. You're not committing to anything yet. You're just letting your mind be free to possibly find solutions you never would have thought of before. Before you do this step, read the beginning of chapter 10 again for my suggestions of the most important changes to make right away.

L is your list of one to three of those action steps that you're willing to commit to and take now.

The final result might look like this:

GOAL

G: My goal is to be ranked in the top 10 next year.

O: Obstacles include: I don't like my coach and he doesn't like me. I hurt my leg last season and I'm still not 100%. I hold back because I'm afraid of hurting myself again. I don't have the money to travel to train with a better trainer.

A: Possible action steps include: I could take Loren's advice and talk to my coach and try to bridge an understanding between us. I could work through my fear, using EFT. I could go back to physical therapy or see an orthopedist for my leg. I could research elite athletes in my sport to see what they do differently from me. I could stop saying I don't have the money and look around for creative ways to train with someone. For instance, I have a lot of cousins in major cities I could stay with while I worked with someone. I could buy that piece of equipment I've had my eye on for months.

L: The action steps I will take right away are:
 1. Talk to my coach.
 2. Practice with EFT, using the sample for fear in the appendix of this book.
 3. Research elite athletes in my sport.

Now you do the same, right now, before you close this book. Give yourself the gift of starting on this new path toward your goal.

All you have to do is begin. As I've said many times, once you make the decision to commit to your goal, opportunities will start to appear.

Try it for yourself and see.

If you would like more help or support, I'm offering a trial month's membership to The Winners Circle Club. See the details on the next page.

Your Trial One-Month Membership to The Winners Circle Club

Congratulations on making the choice to step out of the box, looking for a new approach to improve your performance.

You read this book because you are committed to being the best you can possibly be. Reaching your goals is important to you and you are ready to do everything possible to be a high performer. You stayed with this book because you knew the information here would give you insider tips used by the most successful athletes.

It is your turn to *take decisive action* so I can show you how to build confidence, improve your focus and effectively deal with distractions—plus everything else you need to create a champion mindset.

Now is the time to bridge the gap between what you KNOW and what you DO.

Join Me for Deeper Training

Success is more than just knowing what you are supposed to do. It is about taking action. I am highly dedicated to your success and want to offer you more than I could fit into this book.

Here's what you'll receive during the first month trial:

• Additional training from me via a group phone call twice a month.

• The tools that I and my guest sports performance experts use for winning performance.

• Access to me. During the open Q&A phone call, I will

answer your questions and give you what you need to take your performance to a higher level.

• Audio recordings of the calls to listen to at your convenience.

Got some questions? All you have to do is ask
It's that simple. You ask and I answer. No question is too small or too big or too tough. I promise you, I won't hold anything back. I will freely share what I know about building a champion mindset.

After I give you your answers, I want you to try it out and check back with me on how it worked out. As you put my suggestions into place, we will course correct until we nail it. It's all about implementation and fine-tuning so it works for you. The bottom line is your results. Staying with the program contributes to breakthroughs as you develop your mental game skills.

On the GO
Since you'll be getting a recording of every call, you can listen any time you want. Load them onto your MP3 player, IPod or Smart Phone for easy listening.

So Let's Work Together on
1. Thoughts and beliefs
2. Goals and vision
3. Action Steps
4. Integration
5. And more …

An Additional Special Bonus
I will continue to add new trainings. For instance, if you liked EFT but you're not sure what words to say, you can access my newest video on doing EFT on specific challenges. In fact if you have a specific challenge and want to do EFT on it, let me

know. I might even do a special tapping video on your issue. The videos are like having me do EFT right there with you. I'll tell you what to say, how to do it, and all you have to do is follow along. It's that easy! Just visit http://thewinningpointbook.com to get started.

As you know, a good coach can make the difference in your performance. Well, the same holds true for your mental game. A strong mindset is necessary for optimal performance under pressure. Visit http://thewinnerscircleclub.com to join me for the first month trial. After the first month, I invite you to continue working with me in The Winners Circle Club, an exclusive membership program, to continue learning inside training secrets from the pros. Listen to top coaches, trainers and athletes reveal their strategies for high performance, and continue to receive mindset coaching to develop your mental edge.

Appendix I

EFT Instructions

You possess a variety of beliefs about your performance, abilities and goals that were formed in various ways. Many were absorbed from your surroundings when you were a child before you had the ability to choose your beliefs, and others were formed from experiences you've had since then.

Many of those beliefs work to your advantage. Other beliefs, however, prevent you from performing at your best.

As I said in chapter 6, EFT (Emotional Freedom Techniques) or "tapping" works with acupressure points in the body to help neutralize negative emotions around a specific event and correct the flow of energy. The process makes you conscious of limiting beliefs you have adopted and gives you the freedom to choose new beliefs.

To perform EFT, you tap with your fingertips on various acupressure points on your body as you focus on a particular emotional or physical issue. As you do so, balance is restored, often within minutes. It's sounds simple and easy, and it is. It also works.

Here are the basics for how to use this powerful tool on yourself:

The Tapping Points
The tapping points are at the end of meridians on your body. Meridians are channels for energy where *qi* (chi), circulating

life force, flows through the body. Storing emotions in the body will contribute to imbalance, affecting the flow of energy. Tapping on the end of the meridians helps to balance out disruptions that exist in your energy system. The end points used in the tapping sequence are close to the surface of your body and are easily accessible.

Follow the tapping sequence below and use all of the points. Although two people might be addressing the same issue, the meridian that is blocked can be different for each person due to individual experience and perceptions. By tapping on all of the eight points you are actually accessing every meridian in your body and will hit the block each and every time without having to know which meridian is blocked. The goal is to successfully clear the energy so you can achieve performance results.

Note: When tapping I like to use the four fingertips of my hands on each tapping point, never using my thumbs. I suggest using about the same amount of pressure to tap as if you were drumming your fingers on a tabletop.

The Tapping Sequence:

Karate Chop Point: This is the setup point. Open either hand and with the other hand's fingertips tap on the outside of the open hand between your wrist and pinkie.

Eyebrow Point: This tapping point is located at the beginning of the eyebrow, closest to the center of your face. Put the fingertips of each hand over each eyebrow and tap on the eyebrow using four fingers on each hand.

Side of the Eye: The outer corner of your eye, where the top and lower part meet, is the next tapping point. Use four fingers of both hands on both eyes. Don't get so close to your eye that you are likely to poke it.

Under the Eye: This point is on the cheek under the eye that is even with the pupils. Use both hands and all four fingers. Each

hand is under each eye, tapping on
the bone.

Under the Nose: For this point
you only need one hand. Use all
four fingers to tap above your lip,
with your pointer finger tapping
on the indentation under your nose.

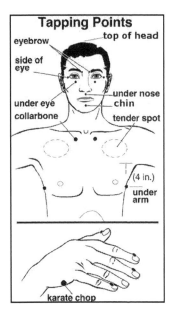

Chin: With this point use only
one hand. Tap in the indentation
between your lower lip and your
chin.

Collarbone: The collarbone
point is the most difficult one to
get correctly. Most people tend to
tap too high up on their collarbone.
Refer to the diagram below. The
correct point is toward the front where your collarbone begins
and then one inch down where you feel an indentation. Once
again, use both hands to tap on each side of your collarbone.

Under the Arms: This tapping point is located about four
inches under the arm pit. Cross your arms when tapping on
this point as if giving yourself a hug. Another variation is to
tap on those points with the fingers of that hand tapping on the
same side of the body. Either way is fine; do whatever is most
comfortable for you.

Top of the Head: This is the final point used to complete the
tapping sequence. With one hand, tap on the crown of your
head.

How to Use the Tapping Sequence:
The Short Cut Method
Part of my approach includes identifying the first event
where a limiting belief might have formed. I then begin to ad-

dress the original circumstance and to shift the perception concerning it. This helps to clear the presenting problem.

For now, however, just think about an obstacle that is affecting your performance. Some suggestions include physical pain, anxieties or not feeling confident. After you choose an issue, try to get very specific about the circumstances under which it occurs.

1. Rate your intensity. Before you start tapping, rate the intensity of that issue for you on a scale from 0 to 10, with ten being the worst.

2. Perform the Setup. While continuously tapping the Karate Chop point only, repeat the affirmation three times:

"Even though I have this [name your obstacle], I deeply and completely accept myself."

3. Do the Tapping Sequence. Now tap about 7 times on each of the energy points above while repeating a reminder phrase at each point. A reminder phrase is a short statement that is related to the setup affirmation.

In the examples and samples that follow, you'll notice that sometimes the reminder phrase changes for each point. That's helpful but not necessary for success. Your reminder phrase can be very simple and stay the same for each tapping point.

Let's do the sequence together (also shown below). For example, say you get nervous right before the start of the race, to the point where you are sick to your stomach. First we'll do the setup together on the karate point chop. You will repeat the setup phrase three times. Then you start tapping on each point while saying a reminder phrase. In the example below, we're repeating "sick to my stomach" while tapping on all the points.

Even though we are keeping it simple, your subconscious is attuned to what is going on and is working with you to calm you down right before the race.

Setup: "Even though I have this sick feeling in my stomach, I deeply love and accept myself." (Repeat three times.)

Eyebrow: sick to my stomach
Side of eye: sick to my stomach
Under eye: sick to my stomach
Under nose: sick to my stomach
Chin: sick to my stomach
Collarbone: sick to my stomach
Under arm: sick to my stomach
Top of head: sick to my stomach

4. Take a deep breath!

5. Rate your ending intensity from 0-10. Are you still at the same number as you began, or did the number change? Did your level of intensity go up or down? See if any specific thoughts, memories or sensations occurred while you were tapping. If so, that is good and seen as progress.

If the intensity is above a "2," repeat the tapping sequence again. If appropriate, you can make the following changes:

• Make the statement more specific; what is the best way to describe what you are feeling now, after the tapping?

• Modify the setup statement to "Even though I still have some of this _____, I deeply and completely accept myself." Using the example above, say you did the sequence and you don't feel quite as sick to your stomach as you did before, but your stomach is still queasy, for this next round of tapping you would say the following setup three times before you begin tapping, "Even though I have this remaining sick-to-my-stomach feeling, I deeply love and accept myself."

• Say a slightly modified reminder phrase as you tap all the points again. For example, your reminder phrase would now be "remaining upset stomach" on each tapping point.

Let's do it together once more.

Setup: Even though I have this remaining sick-to-my-stomach feeling, I deeply love and accept myself. (Repeat three times.)
Eyebrow: remaining upset stomach

Side of eye: remaining upset stomach
Under eye: remaining upset stomach
Under nose: remaining upset stomach
Chin: remaining upset stomach
Collarbone: remaining upset stomach
Under arm: remaining upset stomach
Top of head: remaining upset stomach

A Variation to Try

In the example below, we're using different reminder phrases for each point. If you'd like to try it, think about a performance goal you want for yourself, but feel some kind of resistance or a barrier around it. Notice if you feel the resistance somewhere in your body. Rate your physical or emotional feeling on a scale between 0-10.

Now we are going to tap on the Karate Chop point for the setup. Notice that it's also okay to include variations on the affirmation when you repeat it three times—or you may keep it the same.

This time, after we do the setup, we will do two consecutive rounds of tapping.

Setup:
Even though I continue to have this part of me that resists change, I deeply and profoundly love and accept who I am no matter what.

Even though this vulnerable part of me is satisfied with how things are now and I don't understand this, I accept who I am and how I feel.

Even though I spend a lot of time training and I am not getting the results I expect, I deeply and profoundly accept all of me—even the part that is resisting change and distracts my focus.

Now tap on each point 7 times, using the reminder phrases below.

Eyebrow: Wouldn't it be nice if I could always maintain my focus.

Side of eye: The thought of feeling focused and confident is appealing.

Under eye: I remember a time when I was in the zone and the energy I felt from that.

Under nose: There continues to be a part of me that is comfortable with where I am now.

Chin: I don't understand that part of me.

Collarbone: That is okay.

Under arm: I accept all parts of me right now.

Top of head: I choose to accept every part of me no matter what.

Eyebrow: I appreciate all aspects of who I am.

Side of eye: Even the parts of me that resist and distract my focus.

Under eye: I appreciate how I think and my desire to compete.

Under nose: Even when I lose concentration, becoming distracted.

Chin: I appreciate every single part of me.

Collarbone: Even though the resistance to change is stronger than I would like. Somehow it appears to be protective.

Under arm: I choose to accept all of me.

Top of head: I choose to accept all parts of me no matter what.

Take a deep breath. Check in and see if the number you had has changed. If you felt the resistance in your body somewhere, is it still there? Did it change or move? Any movement is positive even if it became more intense. Movement means change is beginning to happen.

If you are not at a zero level of intensity, I recommend you do the tapping sequence again. As I say above, make it even more specific to the particular issue you have regarding resistance to see if that helps clear it for you.

EFT has the ability to remove the barriers to your progress. Using this process will help you reach your performance goals more easily and quickly. Be skeptical, but give it a try. In fact, try it on everything. The benefit of using the Emotional

Freedom Techniques is the ease of shifting your mindset from negative to positive.

On the following pages are several specific EFT examples you can model as you learn to use the technique.

Again, you'll notice that some of them use different reminder phrases. Feel free to model them or use just one simple reminder phrase.

Tapping diagram is used with permission of Gloria Arenson, MFT, author of *Five Simple Steps to Emotional Healing, Freedom at Your Fingertips,* and *Born To Spend.*

Appendix II

EFT Sample: Physical Pain

I use EFT on myself as well as with clients. Recently, I went skiing with my husband. It was our first day on the slopes for the season and I was eager to use my brand-new skis. I'm an intermediate skier and tend to stick with groomed slopes. Although I know my abilities, I sometimes try to go on ski runs that are advanced just to test my progress.

That weekend was no exception. After several runs on the slopes, I wanted to try one of the advanced, black diamond runs. As soon as I turned to go down the slope I knew I was out of my league. I tried to ski as cautiously as possible, but every time I made a turn I was out of control. I was going too fast, lost my balance and fell. I lost one ski, one ski pole dug deep into the snow, and I felt a crack in my left knee. Fortunately it wasn't broken, but it did hurt a lot, and I was only halfway down the slope.

Even though I usually don't beat myself up, I knew what I did was foolish. Plus, I was hurting and unsure whether I would make it down the mountain. I just didn't know how injured I was.

I could have panicked but, instead, I used EFT. I sat in the snow and began tapping on each of the points.

EFT works even if you can't do it perfectly. For instance, I'm going to fill in the reminder phrases below, but the truth is I don't really remember what I said. I just tapped on the thoughts that came into my head. Also, I know I didn't tap on all the points, because I couldn't reach some of them with my ski jacket and gloves on. I pretty much kept to the points on my face and collarbone.

By the way, this occurred right under the ski lift, but I didn't care who saw me doing this silly tapping thing while sitting in the snow. It was more important to take care of myself than to wonder who might see me.

Below is the setup and simple reminder phrases I could have used for each round of tapping.

Setup: Even though my left knee is hurt, I deeply love and accept myself. (Repeated three times.)
On each point, I could have used the reminder phrase of "my left knee hurts."

Then I could have tapped again, using this:

Setup: Even though I tried skiing on an advanced slope, I deeply love and accept myself. (Repeated three times.)
On each point, the reminder phrase would have been, "skiing on an advanced slope."

Then again:

Setup: Even though it was stupid of me to ski here, I deeply love and accept myself. (Repeated three times.)
On each point, the reminder phrase would have been, "stupid to ski here."

Then finally:

Setup: Even though my left knee hurt and I still need to get down the slope, I deeply love and accept myself. (Repeated three times.)
On each point, the reminder phrase would have been "hurt left knee."

As I sat in the snow, I tapped steadily for about five minutes. The pain gradually receded from an intensity of 10 out of 10 to a 3 and then to a 1. Finally, I began to dig my ski and pole out of the snow, put my ski back on and skied the remainder of that run. At first I thought I was done skiing for the day, but by the time I reached the ski lifts I decided to go for another run on a groomed slope.

Later, as my husband drove, I tapped the entire way home as well as periodically through that evening, focusing on a time I'd fallen off the monkey bars as a child. Current injuries often bring up memories of past injuries and offer an opportunity to clear any blocks around them as well.

I used the setup phrases below.

Setup:
Even though I fell off the monkey bars in elementary school and badly bruised my knee, I deeply love and accept myself.

Even though I couldn't stay balanced on the monkey bars and slipped off of them, I deeply love and accept myself.

Even though I was hanging upside down when I wasn't supposed to, I deeply love and accept myself.

On each of the points I used the same reminder phrase: "monkey bar fall."

Other times I have fallen while skiing, it has taken me several weeks to fully recuperate. This time, however, by the next morning, my pain level was about 2 out of 10.

Once again I began tapping. This time I wanted to tap on my motivation for going down the advanced ski slope.

I began with the setup phrase below:

Even though my left knee hurts, I deeply love and accept myself. (Repeated three times.)

On each point I said the reminder phrase, "My hurt left knee."

Then I tapped again, using this:

Even though I wanted to challenge myself, I deeply love and accept myself. (Repeated three times.)

On each point I said the reminder phrase, "Challenging myself."

Then again:

Even though I had confidence that I could ski down the black diamond, I deeply love and accept myself. (Repeated three times.)
On each point I said the reminder phrase, "Black diamond confidence."

Then finally:

Even though I constantly try to go beyond my comfort level in order to improve my skill, I deeply love and accept myself. (Repeated three times.)
On each point I said the reminder phrase, "Risk-taking fall."

I went to work and started tapping with my clients on their issues. At lunch I had a break. The first thing I noticed was that my knee didn't bother me anymore. My pain level was a 0. I was so excited about this that I called my husband. I continued to feel good with no pain.

The next day my husband, son and I went skiing again. This time I stayed on the intermediate slopes.

Appendix III

EFT Sample to Neutralize Anxiety

One of the biggest complaints about EFT is that it focuses on negative emotions. That is true. Too often people want to tip-toe around negative things because they are uncomfortable. Identifying the negative, saying those words aloud, reduces the intensity of the emotion. The negativity begins to lose its power. It is similar to revealing a deeply held secret you were embarrassed about. Once you share it with someone, and they don't judge you about it, there is a sense of relief. You suddenly feel freedom from something you spent a lot of time avoiding before.

Having said that, I don't like negativity either. So when I use EFT, I do two rounds in consecutive order. First I do a round on the negativity. Then I do a round on the positive, reinforcing the change I am working toward.

We're going to do that together now.

Think of a time when you felt anxiety, even a near-panic, about one of your events. Remember how that distracted you, affecting your performance, and the way your body felt when those thoughts flooded through your head.

Now feel that anxiety as if it is happening right now. Give that anxiety a rating from 0-10, with 10 being a panic attack and 0 being fully relaxed. Do you feel the anxiety in your body? Where? What does it feel like?

While still having those feelings, begin tapping on the Karate Chop point, the side of your hand between your pinky and wrist, for the setup.

If the words I am using are not quite right, substitute your own to fit your experience.

Also, notice that this example uses a more complex style for its reminder phrases.

While tapping on the Karate Chop Point, say these words aloud:

Setup:

Even though I have BIG goals for myself, there is a part of me that is not sure about success, but I deeply love and accept all parts of myself.

Even though I really want to be part of this winning team just as I dreamed, I continue to have this nagging feeling that I don't deserve to be here. Instead, I choose to focus on my gifts and the goals I have set for myself.

Even though I feel selfish focusing on what I want and what I need to be a winner, I truly believe this is the path for me to follow.

Now tap on each of these points as you use these words or you may use the simple phrase of "doubts about success" for each point:

Eyebrow: I know what I would like to have, but is it possible?
Side of Eye: There is so much work I need to do to reach my goal.
Under Eye: I am already overwhelmed.
Nose: I can't add anything else to my plate.
Chin: What if I'm not able to meet their expectations?
Collarbone: I am not really sure I can pull it off.
Under Arm: I don't know if I deserve to be playing with them.
Head: Now is not the time to feel this way. I already feel like I have to do so much to catch up and be accepted.

Now, do it again:

Eyebrow: I can easily imagine being a winner.
Side of Eye: When I stop and think of being a winner, it feels so right.

Under Eye: Being in the moment helps to keep me focused on the BIG picture.

Nose: I choose to embrace the feeling of winning and know I have earned it.

Chin: I have what it takes to be a winner.

Collarbone: It feels so right when I get clear about how I am going to help the team.

Under Arm: Visualizing my success lifts my vibration.

Head: When I feel confident about this path I am taking, my vibration rises and attracts opportunities to me.

Take a deep breath.

Visualize your success. Really see yourself having achieved your goal. Make it as real as you possibly can by bringing all of your senses into play. See it, feel it, be it. Create a champion mindset laser focused on reaching your highest potential.

Appendix IV

EFT Sample: Fear

When I first started rowing, my coach told me I was going to learn to love the burn of going all out in a race. I just chuckled. She had no idea what I thought at the time about pushing my limits or competing.

The truth is, a complete overhaul in my thinking about teamwork and competing was necessary. However, once I made the choice to step out of my comfort zone and give rowing a chance, I also knew change was going to happen.

There was nothing that I could change about the race. What I chose to change was my perception and beliefs about racing. I had to get honest with myself. It was time to figure out what I was avoiding and what was holding me back.

There was a disconnect between what I wanted for myself and how I felt about doing those things. The fear factor was strong. Do you ever feel that way too?

Here is a sample of how to use EFT to vanquish fear.

Think of a time when you felt fear when competing, being expected to do something and you didn't feel you could pull it off. As the thoughts were going through your mind, did you want to run, did you freeze or did you white knuckle your way through?

Now feel that fear as you did when you faced that challenge. Give that fear a rating from 0-10, with 10 being extreme and 0 being confident. What number do you give it? Do you feel it in your body anyplace? Where? What does it feel like?

While still having those feelings we will begin tapping on the Karate Chop point while doing the setup. Again, if the words I am using are not quite right, substitute your own words to fit your experience.

While tapping the Karate Chop Point, the side of your hand between your pinky and wrist, say these words aloud or use your own:

Even though I want to take on the challenge before me right now I know something is holding me back, but I deeply love and accept all parts of myself.

Even though I know what needs to be done to meet the expectations, I have a lot of excuses as to why I can't do it right now. I know this is how I feel and will take action when I am ready.

Even though I am the only one keeping me from taking action and feel the weight of my resistance, I know what I need to do and am working toward the time when I will move forward with confidence and ease.

Now tap on the points while repeating these words:

Eyebrow: I have a self-imposed glass ceiling holding me back from being a high performer.

Side of Eye: I know what I need to do, but am resistant to doing it.

Under Eye: I am afraid to push myself.

Under the Nose: I know all the reasons and excuses for not taking action now.

Chin: There is a price to pay for winning and I am not sure I am willing to pay that price.

Collarbone: What will I have to leave behind if I reach the next level of rankings?

Under the Arms: Just thinking about everything I have to do and what will need to change is overwhelming.

Top of Head: What if I fail?

Again:

Eyebrow: I have the ability to change my focus and look at what I am moving toward.

Side of Eye: I have always had this vision and feel the time is right for making a decision about excellence.

Under Eye: When I visualize reaching my goal, I can feel my energy rise.

Under the Nose: I love the feeling of confidence and achievement I get when I focus on the positive.

Chin: I have so much to offer and now is the time to claim my place with purpose.

Collarbone: I know what I need to do and am ready to do it now.

Under the Arms: My heart and my head are in the right place. I feel really clear about my purpose.

Top of Head: The vibration of being a champion is motivating. I know I have the ability to rise up to and reach any challenge I have created for myself. I love the feeling of confidence as I move forward with purpose.

Take a deep breath.

Change was possible once I knew my goal, my strategy and my plan.

My desire to compete, being a part of the Women's Rowing Team, was greater than my fear. It was time to face it head-on. I had all the tools available to get past my blocks. The opportunity was right to make a change. I had to become comfortable with what had been uncomfortable up until this time.

That's when I embraced the motto: "If it's uncomfortable, then I ought to be doing it."

Being compelled to stretch myself and growing from the decision, created the drive I needed to walk through my fear and resistance. Determination helped me to keep moving forward even when it was uncomfortable.

I reached a point in my life where I could not remain stuck any longer.

Appendix V

EFT and Visualization Exercise

Note: Before doing this exercise, refer to the step-by-step instructions in Appendix I for how to perform EFT.

1. Close your eyes. Breathe deeply and relax your body. Think about an upcoming event that you have some anxiety about or where you want to excel. Include as much detail as possible. What might you see? Where are you standing? Include smells and noises.

Some people are not able to visualize easily. That is okay. Just think about the event in your mind.

2. Now do the EFT setup: while tapping on the side of your palm, say out loud, *Even though I don't feel confident doing this and am afraid that I will fail, I can choose to do this with confidence and ease.* Say it two more times.

3. Then rerun your visualization, imagine yourself doing that activity successfully and tap on all of the points. In your mental dress rehearsal see, hear and feel it happen as you always dreamed it could. See yourself engaged in that activity with confidence and ease. Imagine yourself feeling in control of the event. As you continue tapping, include all the details that could occur at this event and imagine that you are doing them all successfully.

As I said before, when you combine visualization with EFT you get the benefits of both techniques.

While doing the visualization, did you have any doubts or thoughts that you could not do this activity successfully? Maybe you began to feel anxious? That is okay. In fact, it's highly beneficial that you were aware of your doubts and apprehension, because now you can use EFT to neutralize them.

Use EFT to Remove Doubts

If you had any doubts or anxiety arise when you did your visualization, you can use EFT to remove the negative feelings and energy that came up.

1. In this approach, called the Choices Method, you will focus on negative thoughts during the first round, positive thoughts during the second round, and then alternate between negative and positive thoughts on the third round. Model the following example.

Before we begin, let's first have you tune into the challenge and give yourself a rating on its emotional intensity from 0-10 with ten being the most intense and 0 being no intensity whatsoever. Now see if you can feel that emotion in your body anyplace. If so, where do you feel it and what does it feel like? Now let's get tapping, beginning with the setup on the karate chop point, the area on the side of your hand between your wrist and pinky.

First round:

Setup: Even though I feel anxious when I think about doing this and cannot believe that I can do this without anxiety, I choose to do this with confidence and ease.

Even though the thought of doing this makes my heart race and I feel apprehension, I choose to do this with confidence and ease.

Even though it is the thoughts I have about this that make me feel anxious and uncomfortable, I have practiced this successfully in my mental dress rehearsal and choose to do this with confidence and ease.

Eyebrow: This anxiety
Side of eye: This anxious feeling
Under eye: I don't feel I can do this
Under nose: I feel nervous just thinking about it
Under lips: I don't want to do this
Collarbone: I am afraid I'll mess up
Under arms: This familiar nervous feeling
Top of head: I feel anxious at the thought of doing this

Continue tapping a second round:
Eyebrow: I can do this successfully in my imagination
Side of eye: I can see myself doing this with confidence
Under eye: I know what I need to do
Under nose: I have been practicing for this
Under lips: I can do this with confidence
Collarbone: I know what I need to do
Under arms: I am doing the best I can given the circumstances
Top of head: I feel proud that I am willing to change how I feel
about this

Finally tap a third round:
Eyebrow: I am afraid that I will fail
Side of eye: I know what I need to do
Under eye: I will forget what to do
Under nose: I choose to know that I have practiced and rehearsed
for this
Under lips: This familiar nervous feeling
Collarbone: I can see myself doing this successfully
Under arms: I don't want to do this
Top of head: I choose to do this with confidence and ease

Take a deep breath.

Now that you have done all three consecutive rounds check
in to see if your level of intensity has changed at all. Did it go up
or down? Possibly some specific thoughts or memories occurred

while you were tapping. If you are not yet at a zero, I suggest you do all three rounds again. Practice this exercise anytime you have time to relax. When I cured my sugar addiction, I tapped twice a day for ten days. How long it takes varies from person to person. You may notice improvement after the first session, but do give it some time to work.

You can use these techniques in any situation, with any challenge, with any type of memory, whether sports related or not. I tap on everything. Over time you will notice a change in how you view challenges. You will begin to feel more empowered and your outlook will be more positive.

Combining EFT with visualization can help you rise up to any challenge that comes your way and reach your true potential.

Made in the USA
Lexington, KY
20 September 2012